by Groucho-Marxists in Vancouver, Canada • Jacques [
mayoral candidate) in Montréal, Canada by LE • George F
Illinois, USA by Students for Excellence in Education
promoter) in Olympia, Washington, USA • Jean Doré (m
Canada by LE • Helen Chenowith (senator) in Idaho, U
• A World Bank campus recruiter in Brighton, UK by BBB-Brighton Branch
Balcerowicz (neoliberal economist) in Warsaw, Poland • M. Hart-Nibbrich (Dutch
capitalist developer) in Netherlands by GroenFront! • Richard Byrny (chancellor,
University of Colorado) by BBB-Boulder • William Johnson (religious martyr) in
Montréal, Canada by 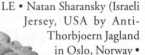 LE • Natan Sharansky (Israeli
minister) in New Jersey, USA by Anti-
Racist Action • Thorbjoern Jagland
(foreign minister) in Oslo, Norway •
Ralph Nader in San Francisco,
California, USA • Ralph Klein
(premier) in Alberta, Canada by
Banana Cream
Three • Raoul Baxter
(president, Smithfield
Foods Europe) in Birmingham,
UK by PETA • Blairo Maggi (governor) in
Mato Grosso, Brazil by Bakers Without
Borders • Bronislaw Geremek (foreign
minister) in Szczecin, Poland by Federacja

PIED

Anarchistyczna • Dimitrios Roussopoulos (authoritarian anarchist publisher) in Montréal,
Canada • Dr. Edward Teller (father of the nuclear bomb) in Los Angeles, California, USA by
Yippies • Sylvia Brustad (Norwegian housing minister) by Bergen Bloetekake Brigade • M.
Thielen (pro-capitalist development Dutch politician) by BBB-Nijmegen • Leif Pagrotsky
(commerce minister), Britta Lejon (democracy minister), & Marit Paulsen (EU-delegate)
simultaneously in Lund, Sweden by Syndicalist Youth Federation • Marguerite Duras (novelist)
in Bruxelles, Belgium by IAP • Clare Short (international development secretary) in Bangor,
Wales by Dim ond Cwstard ("Just Desserts" in Welsh) • Francisco Roher (police captain) in
São Paulo, Brazil • Tsuyoshi Suzuki (sell-out trance dance super DJ) in Matsuri Vortex, South
Africa by HAC-Attack Culinary Criticism Committee • The vice president of Bialystok, Poland
• Helmut Kohl (former chancellor) in Berlin, Germany • Milton Friedman (economist, architect
of neoliberalism) in San Francisco, California, USA by BBB • Michel Camdessus (managing

the Global Pastry Uprising

director, International Monetary Fund) in Bangkok, Thailand by Patissiers San Frontieres • Raël
(messiah & owner, Clonaid and Clonapet, & leader of religious sect that supports cloning &
believes that humans are descendants of aliens) in Montréal, Canada by LE • Ten "Raëliens" in
Montmagny, Canada by LE • Mary Whitehouse (anti-sex, moral crusader) in Brisbane, Australia
• Douglas G. Watson (president & CEO, Novartis), Gordon Rausser (dean, University of
California-Berkeley) & Larry Vanderhoof (chancellor, University of California-Davis)
simultaneously pied in Berkeley & Davis, California, USA by BBB • Frits Bolkestein (right-
wing Dutch politician) in Leiden, Netherlands by TAART • Sir Richard Evans* (chairman,
British Aerospace) in London, UK • Laurette Onkelinx (equality minister, France) by IAP •

continued on page 116

Dedicated to the Cherry Pie 3, who did the crime and served the time.

And to all the folks out there who baked us delicious pies, gave us the heads up and insider information on targets (especially for the Kenneth Derr and Robert Shapiro incidents), funded our missions, let us sleep on their couches, lent us fancy dress clothes for actions, provided invaluable legal/jail support, and helped us in a thousand different ways. Ask not for whom the pie bakes, it bakes for thee.

BIOTIC BAKING BRIGADE
bbb@bioticbakingbrigade.org
www.bioticbakingbrigade.org
Friends of the BBB, POB 40130, San Francisco, CA 94140

〜〜〜〜〜〜〜〜〜〜〜〜〜〜〜〜〜〜〜〜〜〜〜

This book was co-edited and designed by a member of the hella-cool *Earth First! Journal* collective. If you like this publication, you'll definitely want to check them out.

EARTH FIRST! JOURNAL
collective@earthfirstjournal.org
www.earthfirstjournal.org
POB 3023, Tucson, AZ 85702

photo/art credits given when known. cover photo by James Connolly.

Pie Any Means Necessary

artwork by Agent Custard

The Biotic Baking Brigade Cookbook

Pie Any Means Necessary—
The Biotic Baking Brigade Cookbook
ISBN: 1-902593-88-X
© 2004 AK Press
First AK Press/Rebel Folk Press edition

Library of Congress Control Number: 2003113037

AK Press
674-A 23rd Street
Oakland, CA 94612-1163
USA
(510) 208-1700
www.akpress.org
akpress@akpress.org

AK Press
PO Box 12766
Edinburgh, EH8 9YE
Scotland
(0131) 555-5165
www.akuk.com
ak@akedin.demon.uk

**The addresses above would be delighted to provide you
with the latest complete AK catalog, featuring several
thousand books, pamphlets, zines, audio products,
video products, and stylish apparel published & distrib-
uted by AK Press. Alternatively, check out our websites
for the complete catalog, latest news and updates,
events, and secure ordering.**

~~~~~~~~~~~~~~~~~~~~~~~~~~

Published in association with:

Rebel Folk Press
www.rebelfolk.org
whatup@rebelfolk.org

FORWARD!

As multinational corporations accelerate the plunder of our world, a militant resistance has formed in response. Diverse in philosophy and targets, diffuse in geography and structure, the movement comprises freedom-loving folks with a sense of aplomb and gastronomics. Fighting a guerrilla media and ground war with the titans of industry, these revolutionary bakers and pie-slingers have achieved in short order what can truly be called a Global Pastry Uprising (GPU).

This uprising has its roots in the belief that our planet is not dying, it is being killed; and the ones doing the killing have names and faces. Since the GPU began in the late 20th century, dozens of prominent corporate executives, politicians, economists, and sell-out non-governmental organization "leaders" have received their just desserts for crimes against people and the land. When it comes to defending the Earth from the corporate universe, the pie's the limit!

In *Pie Any Means Necessary: The Biotic Baking Brigade Cookbook*, our militant bakers share what they have learned about every aspect of pie-slinging, from the practical to the theoretical, from arcane history to today's proud purveyors of palatable projectiles. The following pages contain essential tips on planning and strategy, as well as recipes, songs, verses, and frontline accounts of the most outstanding deliveries.

A Spanner in the Gears

As the Zapatistas have made clear, in a global economy, we all live in Chiapas. The Biotic Baking Brigade (BBB) builds on that connection: Under *neoliberalismo*, we can all throw a pie in the face of economic fascism. No bosses, offices, foundation grants, never-ending consensus meetings, or CMLA's (Confusing Multi-Letter Acronyms) are needed. As the Nike corporation says: "Just Do It!"

Pie-slinging is just one tool in a large toolbox of resistance to the dominant

ARD!

paradigm. We have utilized diverse tactics across the spectrum of resistance to effect positive change, and will continue to do so. Pieing has broadened the scope of protest, instead of replacing other methods. Having said that, we also believe that it's far better to pie on our feet than to live on our knees.

No Pastry, No Peace!

BBB agents are often experienced activists involved in ecology, social justice, animal rights, anti-racist, and feminist movements, who participate in groups such as Earth First!, Food Not Bombs, and ACT UP. They see interrelationships between different movements, instead of relagating themselves to single issue ghettoes. The diversity of pie victims on the "Tried and Pied" list reflects the fact that it's impossible to have a healthy environment without social justice. Likewise, we can't have a sustainable society without intact ecosystems.

An objective observer cannot dispute that the global market has brought the planet to the brink of economic collapse and that the export-oriented "free trade" model has been devastating for people and the environment alike. Since the BBB directs most of our efforts toward

photo by Adrian Arbib

ecological issues, some have wondered what the mayor of San Francisco had to do with the environment. By pieing him and speaking out during the subsequent media blitzkrieg, the Cherry Pie 3 (as they came to be called) demonstrated through their personal backgrounds in social/eco/animal issues that what we have in front of us is one struggle, one fight.

Speaking Pie to Power

An advantage to our form of dissent is that pie-throwing enjoys an illustrious history... It's as American as apple pie. Satire has always been one of the best weapons of the dispossessed, as the widespread public support for this brand of pielitical pressure shows.

Pie puns aside, there is a serious nature to this comical act. Describing their recent pastry attack on a genetic engineer in England, the *Biotech* Baking Brigade stated, "We are against monoculture and for biodiversity, against the domestication of people and land, and for the wild. There is no neutral ground: everyone is called upon to choose their side. They have declared war on us and our planet: we will answer it."

The technocrats who dominate industrial society may call us radical and unrealistic, but the dream of a biodiverse and socially just future is one that we will fight for until the day we pie.

From the mountains of the Californian Northwest,

—AGENT APPLE FOR THE BBB

Two members of the National Pies Association (NPA) commit ritual public pieicide. The NPA, a mysterious group that surfaced in San Francisco when the pie wars erupted in the Fall 1998, protested the harsh treatment of arrested BBB agents. At their first public appearance, they burst into a Chamber of Commerce leadership seminar, "shouted 'death to all tyrants' in Latin and English, and smashed pies into their own faces... then walked out defiantly without a further word." Membership in the NPA was open to anyone who would raise their left hand and repeat: "They can have my pie when they pry my bloated, overweight fingers from it."

BY DAVID ROVICS

See the man in his li-mo-sine In his tie and
well-pressed shirt Hop-ing that he's
not been found on the look-out for de-sert
He knows that he is guil-ty And a
vi-sit might be paid By the ve-gan
vi-gi-lan-tes of the bi-o-tic bak-ing-bri-
gade What's that sail-ing through the
air In the board-rooms see them shi-ver You can
spend your life hop-ing for pie in the sky but the
bak-ing bri-gade de-li-vers

If you sell your city's soul
To the landlords' greedy pack
You, my friend, have earned yourself
A tasty pastry snack
You can call yourself a liberal
And hope your crimes will fade
But your sell-out soul will be exposed
By the Biotic Baking Brigade

Chorus

So if you cut down the last of the forests
Spew poison in the air
Don't you be surprised to find
That cheesecake in your hair
Yes if you are a corporate criminal

You've surely made the grade
To receive a fresh-baked goody from
The Biotic Baking Brigade

Chorus

Beware all you scoundrels of industry
We know of your disgrace
So smile for the camera
With the cream pie in your face
You can hope that we won't find you out
As you're hiding in the shade
But someday soon you'll live to meet
The Biotic Baking Brigade

Chorus

"Entarteurs" Take Note: Custard Wins Test of Best Pies for Throwing

—THE *WALL STREET JOURNAL*, MAY 26, 1999

LONDON—It's hard enough remembering to pick up eggs and milk at the store, but imagine also trying to decide whether a custard or lemon meringue pie would be more appropriate to throw at someone's face.

One of Britain's largest supermarket chains, Tesco PLC, says it has seen a surge in customer requests for the perfect pie to throw. In response, the company decided to test its pies by tossing them at employees. Safety was a main concern.

"We like to keep abreast of what the customers are doing, and that's why we have had the testing," says Tesco spokeswoman Melodie Schuster. "But at the end of the day it's our food, and we have to look at the food-safety aspect of this sudden craze."

Tesco's pies performed admirably in the air. "All our pies seem to fly extremely well," Mrs. Schuster says. "When you throw them and they land on someone, they make a nice, clean mess." The company recommends three of its pies for throwing—egg custard, lemon meringue and fruit.

Tesco says customer interest in pie throwing has increased because of high-profile stunts such as the attack by "entarteurs" on Microsoft Corp. Chairman Bill Gates last year in Brussels. Pie sales also spiked after an episode of *The Simpsons* featured pie throwing.

Tesco tested its pies several weeks ago by bringing workers from its purchasing, technology, and product-development departments to a school gymnasium near its headquarters in Hertfordshire, about 20 miles north of London. After plastic was spread across the floor, employees stood behind a table and threw dozens of pies at other employees from about four feet away. Still other workers recorded whether pies "splattered in the right way and landed nicely," Mrs. Schuster says. It was important that pies "not make an absolute mess, but a nice, polite mess."

For the best in value and splatter, staffers recommend egg custard, at about $1.65 a pie. "The custard tart gives total face coverage," says Mrs. Schuster.

The lemon meringue also performs well, holding together nicely in flight. "The crunchy outer layer, upon hitting the victim, first of all will crack," she says, "and then the lemony filling will break up and cover the face, leaving a yellow smear." For a more colorful effect, Tesco recommends its fruit pies, but it discourages throwing its frozen pies because they won't splatter.

Mrs. Schuster is unsure whether Tesco will conduct more tests, but it is considering offering customers a pamphlet explaining how to remove pie stains from clothes.

Theory and History

"Never doubt that a small and dedicated group of people with pies can change the world. Indeed, it is the only thing that ever has."

—MARGARET MEAD

Delicious Mischief

BY JUDE ABBOTT

In recent years, members of the BBB have thrown lovingly baked organic pies into the faces of some of the world's most powerful and famous people. They call it "pie-rect action." It is catching on fast: There have been dozens of verifiable pieing incidents around the world during the last few years, with a global flurry of interest from South Africa to Chile and Australia to Burma.

The BBB describes itself as "an underground network of militant bakers who deliver just desserts to those in power." Their philosophy is forthright. They believe that the future of the planet is threatened by a worldview that puts profit, trade, and share values above life itself. Rather than wait for politicians and bureaucrats to tackle these issues, the BBB has taken on the challenge themselves with organic home-baked pastries, vegan custard, and that late 20th century, nutritionally void, environmentally wasteful decorative product: whipped cream in an aerosol can. They publicly throw pies into the faces of people they identify as powerful, unaccountable, and responsible for crimes against the planet. They stand against "industrial society in all its forms, against neoliberalism and technocracy, and against corporate crooks and their allies in government." They stand for "ecology, bioregionalism, human-scale economies—and proper gastronomics."

The BBB is part of a tradition of making a point through a prank. Pie-throwing has a proud lineage traceable back through Jerry Lewis, Wile E. Coyote, the Marx Brothers, and yippies such as Abbie Hoffman. It can be seen in the same context as the Dadaists and Surrealists who sent insulting letters to challenge the pretensions of worthlessly famous people. In fact, pieing can be traced back to court jesters, part of whose roles were to belittle royalty or powerful people.

Pieing is but one creative tool in the toolbox of resistance. Culture jamming is another. In general, activists seem to be looking to be more creative in their endeavors. Opponents of the current system are disillusioned with traditional channels of dissent—writing letters, voting, complaining, and being ignored. Disenchanted people have often felt that their only option has been to join a political party where others would think and take action on their behalf, as well as to tell them what to do—which has often been an equally disempowering experience. A lot of current activism aims to provoke thought and to get people doing things for themselves again. This despite the often-leveled accusations of current political apathy. Actually, it's just party politics we're all tired of.

The term "culture jamming" was originally coined in 1984 by the San Francisco audio-collage band Negativeland. The practice of culture jamming—parodying advertisements and altering billboards in order to drastically change the message—was an ingenious way of using a company's own advertising as a weapon against itself.

"A good jam, in other words," says author Naomi Klein, "is an X-ray of the subconscious of a campaign, uncovering not an opposite meaning but a deeper truth hidden beneath the layers of advertising euphemisms. According to these principles, with a slight turn of the imagery knob, the now-retired Joe Camel turns into Joe Chemo hooked up to an IV machine. That's what is in his future, isn't it?"

Culture jamming also includes media activism, such as burning a heap of television sets in front of CBS's Manhattan offices as part of a protest against media bias during the 1991 Gulf War (a protest that was staged by Fairness and Accuracy in Reporting). A somewhat more conventional, but no less valid, strain of culture jamming is mediawatch projects such as Paper Tiger Television, an independent collective that produces programs that comment on the information industry. There is also Not Channel Zero, a collective of young African American "camcorder activists" whose motto is "The Revolution, Televised."

Culture jammers, like the BBB and other entarteurs, are Groucho Marxists, aware of the fun to be had in the joyful smashing of authoritarian ideologies. As Jello Biafra once observed, "There's a big difference between 'simple crime' like holding up a 7-11 and 'creative crime' as a form of expression. Creative crime is uplifting to the soul. What better way to survive our anthill society than by abusing the very mass media that sedates the public? A prank a day keeps the dog leash away!"

Jude Abbott plays a wicked horn with Chumbawamba, www.chumba.com.

RULES OF CRUMB

The BBB is often asked all sorts of questions related to the practical aspects of pie-throwing: how to choose a target, slip past security, deliver the goods, fight the legal system, etc. The following is a compilation of what we've learned through the (dessert) course of our struggle.

Aim High...

Several field agents recently reflected on the amazing array of successful pie operations since the GPU began. Aside from splooshing the heads of the unholy neoliberal triumvirate (World Trade Organization, International Monetary Fund, and World Bank) and the CEOs of Monsanto, Novartis, Enron, Chevron, and Maxxam, there have also been the heads of state (Canada, Poland, and Ireland), as well as cabinet ministers and members, senators, and mayors worldwide. Amazing! Who woulda thunk it was possible? This campaign is a testament to the armed forces slogan: "Be All You Can Be." The BBB and others have shown that it pays to go for the gusto when it comes to pie-slinging and aim high.

...and Just Do It!

Magic happens when it comes to pieing and other forms of direct action. Ed Abbey once wrote that sentiment without action is the ruin of the soul. As we like to say, "A rolling pin gathers no moss." Once you put your mind and body into motion in defense of what's right, the universe opens up opportunities that would normally seem impossible. Yet, it's important to also remain flexible and simply allow oneself to be propelled by events instead of forcing them.

1. Dress for Success

Whether dinner-dancing at the Copacabana or creaming the head of a major multinational corporate criminal enterprise, your attire can often make or break the event. The well-dressed pie-thrower will enjoy a host of advantages over her poorly-garbed, dread-headed, skanky eco-freak friend. This is not to make a value judgment—some of our best friends fall into the latter category—it's just to say that there's a time and a place for everything. Shave, put on a suit, keep your hair short, and you can go anywhere.

Of course, there are always exceptions. In the case of the Charles Hurwitz pie incident, the pastry assailant was dressed like the corporate executive's worst hippie nightmare. Nevertheless, the spirit was with the pie-slinger that day, and the pie met its mark. As he said afterward, "I'm merely a vessel through which the holy spirit flows."

If you feel comfortable with your dress and armaments, and if you can translate that into an attitude and look of belonging in a particular place, the world is your *tarte classique*. The BBB is often asked how we get into high security events, and the answer is that along with a few practical details and sincere prayers, it's shockingly easy.

2. Don't Forget to Fortify Yourself

"Blend into the crowd, adopt a pleasant, civilized demeanor—and if someone offers you a glass of nice red wine... accept it graciously. Historically, booze has often been featured in pastry attacks, primarily because it helps relieve the pre-pie jitters but also because it serves admirably as inspiration. According to Belgian pie prankster Noël Godin, who spearheaded the Bill Gates pieing in

Brussels in February 1998, beer was instrumental in both the planning and execution stages of the attack." —*San Francisco Weekly*

3. Ready, Aim...

Whenever it is possible, the BBB uses vegan whipped cream on paper plates for maximum sploosh effect, as well as the fact that paper plates are the safest possible launch vehicles. However, this is often not possible because of the high level of security surrounding our targets. For example, one of our counterparts in London failed in his attempt to flan the chairman of British Aerospace because as the pastry assailant approached the stage, he had to stop and fill a plate with whipped cream. At this point, security was able to intercept and detain him. He was kicked out of the event with no charges pressed.

Consider if our man had instead sauntered casually up to the stage with a smart-looking attaché case and at the last minute pulled out a vertically placed tofu creme missile—Splaaamo! Large notebooks have also been used to successfully conceal edible missiles.

Another proven tactic is to place a pie in a pizza box with a round cut-away in the bottom and a delightful bouquet of flowers on the top to cover the box. You can approach your target with a loving smile, then in a heartbeat remove the pie through the bottom and let fly. Nothin' says lovin' like somethin' from the oven.

Again, the purpose of a pie-in-the-face of a scoundrel is to hurt his/her image and ego, not their physical person. That's because a legitimate target depends more on his image and public persona than her actual self. Second, if the target is physically hurt, it will often detract from the message of the action itself, and the pie-thrower, if caught, will usually get hammered by the law.

A pie is clearly an ineffective weapon compared to, say, a brick or a bar stool, and one should use appropriate tools at appropriate times. We're all for appropriate technology, but in the GPU, the foremost goal is to damage a person's image. In today's global economy, that is our target's most important asset.

Therefore, we recommend that when a target is wearing glasses, unless you have whipped cream on a paper plate, a very fluffy pie, or a steady arm and a clear line of fire, do not pie them straight in the face. This is not to say that other strategies haven't been employed successfully: Les Entartistes of Montréal have delivered full facial coverage using aluminum plates with great *élan* and effectiveness. But as pastry combat veterans, we've come to feel that the risk of breaking someone's glasses and injuring their eyes is not worth it, considering that a pie agent could instead deliver a striking sploosh to the target's head, cheeks, collar/tie, or perhaps even groin. As the great political theorist Bob Marley once said, "He who lives to run away, comes back to pie another day."

In closing, while it may be tempting for enterprising first-time pie-slingers to wallop a deserving crook smack in the kisser with the cream of righteousness (in other words, to smash the pie in the target's face), we would urge caution given that the act of throwing the pie is significant in and of itself, regardless of where or whether it hits the mark or how hard.

4. Special Air Service

A passionate debate rages among entartistas regarding the question of whether to throw the edible missile or to mush it in the recipient's face. Frankly, our group is split on this issue. On the one hand, an airborne fusillade is such an amazing sight, and the sound of a long-distance splat elicits tears of joy to us pie-throwers. On the other hand, if one misses with a toss, it's such a grievous bummer. To plant a pie directly on the target is a much more certain bet. We recommend target practice for all field agents to decide what works best for them, though circumstances may determine the method.

For instance, there were plans afoot for several weeks to flan a certain foreign head of state when he came to our neck o' the woods. This corrupt scumbag is doing his best to crush an indigenous uprising and install neoliberal economics *Über Alles*, and we felt he needed his just desserts, BBB-style. Security was going to be Intense with a capital I, so we figured the best we could do (while not getting shot) was a medium to long distance toss. For reasons we can't disclose without compromising an agent, the action didn't

come off as planned, but we did come to believe that the big heave-ho was a valid tactic—especially since it would have been an international incident even if it missed!

Agent Lemon Custard suggests making it clear that you're throwing a pie if there are armed bodyguards present by keeping the delicious weapon held high, in addition to avoiding lunges and quick movements. She's found that a steady, confident approach keeps bodyguards lulled into complacency and offers the best chance for successful delivery. If you can get near the target, he/she probably won't be able to escape from you, thus you might be able to take it slower than you think. However, it should be said that the element of surprise is often the only way to achieve full facial treatment.

Sometimes one will want to make a statement before launching the creamy fusillade. Before Milton Friedman met his fate, the entartista was heard to say, "Mr. Friedman, it's a good day to pie!" San Francisco Mayor "Slick Willie" Brown heard "Matrix this!," eco-spy Barry Clausen was told "Mr. Clausen, that's assault!," and Chevron CEO Kenneth Derr was questioned: "Do people really die for oil? People Do [splat]!" (a reference to Chevron's "People Do" ad campaign).

As for how many people to include in a particular action, there are several factors to consider. It might be easier to remain inconspicuous and reach the target with only one or two pie-slingers. Then again, if a diversion is worked out and everyone's attention is drawn to one direction, then an agent can usually approach from the opposite direction with remarkable ease. There is also the *kamikaze* (Japanese for "divine sploosh") technique, most clearly demonstrated through the Willie Brown and Bill Gates incidents, in which the pastry assailants came in from every angle and descended upon their prey in a mad burst of speed and passion.

5. Intent to Pie

There are different intentions with every pie toss, based on the pie-er, the pie-ee, and the situation/location. For instance, being pied can be considered a compliment. Jean Chrétien, the premier of Canada, said as much: "It's a great honor for anyone to get pied." Of course, that was before he was actually pied in August 2000—afterward he felt differently! Hoops Harrison, national director of the Canadian Alliance of Student Associations, concurred with the following post-pie remark: "I don't really mind; a lot of cool people have gotten pied."

One BBB agent said, "I myself have been pied five times, sometimes by surprise and other times by consent. Who says we can dish it out but can't take it? My only request is that the pie is a tasty, organic, and vegan treat."

Other pie-tossings are acts of rage or revenge. Thousands of pies are thrown every year, from causes as varied as fundraisers for elementary schools to birthday pranks for geriatric tricksters with an epicurean bend. The only constant in the equation is the joy that a proper gloup delivers, but every other factor is subject to change depending on the intent of the pie-thrower.

6. The Pies Themselves

It should be noted that the BBB dishes up homemade pies whenever time permits, and after that, quality desserts from local bakeries. In emergencies, we've picked up confections from a gas station. Pie any means necessary.

We've found that there is a special, symbiotic relationship we create by baking a pie that we then deliver. It's kind of like growing and eating your own food, there's something very special and do-it-yourself style about it that you can't get through shopping.

We've also found it quite delightful to employ a wide variety of pies, tarts, crumbles, flans, jelly donuts, and other treats in our arsenal. It gives the media a story hook onto which we can hang our message. One concern, however, is to not let the focus stray too far from the point of the pieing into all of the slapstick details. It's a tough balance to achieve. Often it is out of our control, but if at first you don't succeed, pie pie again.

One lesson learned from the Willie Brown pie incident is that a mixed berry pie (the media called it cherry pie) at first glance looks a lot like blood on a person's face. If that is not the intended effect, and it usually isn't, then we recommend sticking with more conventional flavors. It may, however, be a great choice for a homophobic preacher or neo-Nazi Klansman.

Achieving the perfect consistency for full facial coverage is a matter of great delicacy. If the pastry is too hard, it will not sploosh. If it is too soft, it will be difficult to transport without spilling all over. See our recipe section to learn how to bake the perfect item for a "special air service."

7. Justice or Just Us? Pies and the Law

Anyone following the GPU, or just plain paying attention to the current political climate, should know that the following maxim may apply: Use a Pie, Go to Jail. If one goes after a politician or businesswoman on stage at a public event (which is usually the best time to do so), the odds may be against a successful delivery and escape. Let's call this the "pie high" technique.

Whereas, with the "pie-and-fly" technique, the odds of escape improve greatly. We employ this method usually when our agents can't afford to get caught (for legal or other reasons) or when the target is worthwhile to pie but not if you have to go through the legal grinder. The secret to this method is to attack when they least expect it. Two of the best examples were both Bill Gates and Kenneth Derr getting splattered as they each left their chauffeured cars and approached the entrances to buildings.

The field agents involved in an operation have two major considerations in deciding which route to go: Is it worth it to strike at the moment when the target is most visible, thus achieving the greatest coverage of the event (the Gates and Brown incidents were played repeatedly to millions of viewers around the world on CNN as well as on local television networks)? If so, can the operatives accept the consequences, legal and otherwise, which may accompany a pie action?

The penalties for pie-throwing are extremely varied, depending on the identity of the victim, the identity of the pie-thrower, the type of event where the incident occurred, the details of the pie delivery, the reaction of the victim, the current political climate (in regard to the specific issue at hand if there is one or the political climate in general), the quality of the lawyer if you choose to be represented, etc.

Sometimes the cops will laugh, congratulate the pie-thrower, and no charges will be pressed. Other times, it will be treated like the current standard-fare of protest, such as an office occupation or road blockade. The harshest punishment we've heard of for pieing is the six-month maximum jail sentences received by the Cherry Pie 3, of which they served four before being released for "good behavior." Salmon Soufflé Society pie-thrower Randall Mark, who flanned US Senator Helen Chenowith in Idaho, was also sentenced to six months because he was on probation for an anti-logging protest. Others have had fines and long probation terms. The best attitude to have is: Don't let the police state keep ya down, but at the same time, don't expect justice.

8. Jail

Whilst in the clink, one can still be very active, a strategy we in the industrial world often neglect. See page 87 for an example on how to do this.

9. Guerrilla Media

If he were alive today, Sun Tzu would have claimed in his text *The Art of War* that the twofold way of the modern warrior is no longer that of the sword and pen, but rather the pie and keyboard. We've found few things as effective to subvert an event (shareholders' meetings, legislative hearings, press conferences, keynote speeches, etc.) as a well-placed pie and a captivating press release.

Corporate media outlets present a spectacle that bamboozles and distracts viewers. To state the obvious, it is extremely difficult to get a dissenting message through these media filters and into the hearts and minds of the public. If we hold a rally in demonstration-jaded San Francisco, the media usually will not cover it. If we write letters to the editor, they don't get printed. However, the visual of a pie in the face makes a sizable chink in the media armor through which we can then put forth the reasons why a figure deserved to be pied in the first place. It allows us to communicate our message beyond what traditional means allow.

That is not to say that we should only rely on mass media. We actively support alternative media and do what we can to create our own. The largest

slice of the pie, in terms of energy spent on press work, should go to creating and supporting alternative media. One way we've been able to do this, following the lead of the Zapatistas, is through the strategic use of the Internet to bypass the corporate media filters and deliver our words straight to the people. Another route has been a fruitful alliance with the culture-jamming group Whispered Media, www.whisperedmedia.org. It acquires footage of our pie-tossings and then distributes video and still-images far and wide. The group also produced a brilliant documentary on the GPU, *The Pie's the Limit*, which is shown at gigs both in North America and abroad, as well as on the tube.

Two grassroots how-to media publications deserve special mention: *The Ruckus Society's Media Manual*, www.ruckus.org, and *An Activists' Guide to Exploiting the Media*, www.videonetwork.org/media.html.

If the job is done right, a group can achieve massive media "market saturation" through a surprisingly small amount of work. A few key components are to get video and stills to the television networks and news wire services quickly (Associated Press and Reuters in particular), put together a witty and tight press release ahead of time so that it's ready to go out immediately after the action, and to have one or more agents available at an office or on a cell phone to do interviews at the phone number put on the press release. These three points cannot be overstated. An email address should also accompany phone numbers at the top of the press release.

Ultimately, the corporate media will co-opt our message of dissent when it becomes effective enough to make people think. Therefore, we all need to create alternative means of communication, as well as to support those already in existence—such as radical publications and pirate/community radio.

An example of appropriately rejecting the corporate media occurred when the BBB turned down an interview in December 1998 with ABC's "Good Morning America" in order to support the corporation's 2,200 locked-out workers. An injury to one is an injury to all.

Lastly, the liberal activist belief that "if you don't do media, you get done by the media" is a load of bollocks. The point of direct action is the action itself, not pandering to the corporate press and letting it dictate your strategy. If you want to do media then that's swell, and if you get the kind of press you want that's even better. But make sure that whatever you do, do it with all your heart and leave concerns about the globalized media spectacle behind.

"Canada's recent bout of culinary terrorism has the Royal Canadian Mounted Police (RCMP) worried. Is the nation experiencing a rise in civil disobedience not seen since the Vietnam War protests three decades ago? The assault on Prime Minister Jean Chrétien 'clearly indicates that the proponents of civil disobedience have permeated all levels of our society and even a law-abiding city such as Charlottetown, Prince Edward Island cannot be considered a low-risk venue'."

—THE *VANCOUVER SUN* REGARDING A SEPTEMBER 2000 REPORT BY RCMP COMMISSIONER GUILIANO ZACCARELLI, OBTAINED UNDER THE FREEDOM OF INFORMATION ACT

The Theory of Pie

BY AUDREY VANDERFORD

The rich and powerful: corporate executives, government officials, economists, bioengineers. They live their lives sheltered by secretaries, security guards, public relations officials, chauffeurs, police. They appear in public only briefly at $1,000 per plate dinners and black tie functions. Surrounded by their supporters and their peers, they remain isolated from the public and from dissent.

And then, "gloup!"

Through all the barriers the elites have erected around themselves sails the cream pie. Its filling drips and oozes, smearing their pristine presentation, staining their suits, injuring their pride, and momentarily cracking their facade of omnipotence. Always on the heels of corporate and political celebrities, the media cameras click and whirl, broadcasting the image worldwide. We witness one of those rare moments when justice is indeed served.

Political Pranks and the Laughter of the People

The "pie-in-the-face" prank has a lengthy history with manifestations in popular and folk culture. Like most pranks, pies are acts of ritualized inversion and humiliation. They draw on the power of laughter to unsettle and disrupt. Political pie-throwers carefully craft the symbolism in their pranks, something evident in both the enactment and in the subsequent discussion and documentation of the pie.

Any successful prank is a nuanced and well-crafted event, executed with strategic planning and with anticipated results. When combined with elements of parody and political wit, a prank can offer an entertaining act of social criticism. Pranks operate on and through power dynamics, inverting structures of status and convention. According to journalists V. Vale and Andrea Juno, a prank connotes *fun, laughter, jest, satire, lampooning, making a fool of someone*—all light-hearted activities. Thus do pranks camouflage the sting of deeper, more critical denotations, such as their direct challenge to all verbal and behavioral routines. They undermine the sovereign authority of words, language, visual images, and social conventions in general. Regardless of the specific manifestation, a prank is always an evasion of reality. Pranks are the deadly enemy of reality. And "reality"—its description and limitation—has always been the supreme control trick used by a society to subdue the lust for freedom latent in its citizens.

Frequently dismissed as child's play, pranks can in fact be dramatic folk traditions, comically subversive performances, radical street theater. Political pranks draw on a long history found in both literature and performance.

In his book *Rabelais and His World*, Mikhail Bakhtin examines popular forms of laughter and humor in the Middle Ages, focusing in particular on the world of carnival as depicted in the novels of François Rabelais. According to Bakhtin, medieval society was divided into two distinct spheres—the official and the carnival worlds. While the former was characterized by hierarchy, stability, morality, and dogma, the latter provided a reprieve from these rules. "One might say," writes Bakhtin, "that carnival celebrated temporary liberation from the prevailing truth and from the established order. It marked the suspension of all hierarchical rank, privileges, norms, and prohibitions." During carnival, the sacred was blasphemed and the nobility mocked; it was a "world inside out" and upside down. The laughter of carnival, contrary to the seriousness and drudgery of official life, was uninhibited and replete with excessive and grotesque imagery—wine, sex, food, the "material bodily lower stratum." All this, Bakhtin argues, had a different connotation in the Middle Ages than it does today. Rather than being merely negative or "gross," this type of bodily humor was inseparable from the regenerative meanings of birth and growth. This transformative impulse of carnival allowed people to enter, for a time, "the utopian realm of community, freedom, equality, and abundance."

Although Bakhtin argues that laughter has changed since the time of Rabelais and has lost much of its regenerative power, he also states that "the popular-festive carnival principle is indestructible." Arguably political pie-throwing taps into this principle, as it seeks to dethrone the powerful and engages the laughter of the people. Pie-throwing is what Bakhtin calls "carnivalesque." As Graham Chapman of Monty Python quips: "Nothing can equal the ribald connotations of an edible missile."

"The Pie is Cast:" The History of Pie-Throwing

From the pie-toss at the county fair to vaudeville, stage, and screen, shoving a pie in someone's face has been a common act of slapstick and subversion. As Mack Sennett, founder of the Keystone Cops proudly declared, "A pie in the face, provided that the recipient does not anticipate it, has no equal in slapstick comedy. It can reduce dignity to nothing in seconds." Contemporary prankster activists combine this traditional custom with *political* targets and innovative press releases. Pies are retributive pranks, punishing corporate criminals, corrupt government officials, and others who exploit and oppress.

Pie-throwing became an expression of political discontent in the late '60s and early '70s with the yippies. Aron Kay, known as "the Pieman," tossed pies at numerous politicians and public figures, including anti-feminist Phyllis Schlafly, Watergate "plumber" G. Gordon Liddy, Senator Daniel Patrick Moynihan, and artist Andy Warhol. Kay retired in 1992 after pieing Randall Terry, head of the anti-abortion group "Operation Rescue." Today, he maintains a website that contains photographs and descriptions of his "pie-litical" acts, as well as updates on the actions of others.

Political pie-throwing in Europe also has its origins in the '60s. Noël Godin is infamous throughout Europe for his numerous pie-pranks. Godin was active in the student uprisings in Paris. "I was never cured of the fever of May 1968," he admits. Godin continues to subscribe to the situationist practice of *détournement:* the "theft" of pre-existing artistic productions and their integration into a new construction, one that serves a radical political agenda. According to the situationists, an anarchist group instrumental in the events of May '68, *détournement* provides a disruption or fracture in the "spectacle" of modern capitalist representations.

In February 1998, Godin along with fellow "entarteurs" from the Patisserie Brigade Internationale showered the king of capitalism, Microsoft Chairman Bill Gates, with nearly 25 pies (four of which reached their intended target). The Gates incident drew significant media attention and to a certain degree re-ignited interest in this form of culinary activism. Godin explained that his "gang of bad hellions who have declared the pie war on all the unpleasant celebrities in every kind of domain" pied Gates because "he is the master of the world. He's offering his intelligence, his sharpened imagination, and his power to the governments and to the world as is today—that is to say gloomy, unjust, and nauseating. He could have been a utopist, but he prefers being the lackey of the establishment. His power is effective and bigger than that of leaders of governments, who are only many-colored servants. So Bill Gates was at the top of our lists of victims. The attack against him was symbolic; it was against hierarchical power itself."

In 1997, six months before Gates was pied, the BBB struck one of their first targets: Charles Hurwitz—CEO of Maxxam Corporation, parent company of Pacific Lumber—who is responsible for the clearcutting of the Headwaters old-growth redwood forest in northern California. Although many of the BBB pieings that would follow occurred in the San Francisco Bay area, they now have "factions" worldwide. They are adamant, however, that they are not a formal organization; they are "flan-archists." As a BBB spokesperson notes, "The BBB is a movement rather than a group. We have no members, though there is an underground network of militant bakers who provide us with nothing but the best vegan and organic pies. The focus of the current pastry 'uprising' is to hold corporate crooks and their lackeys in government and the nonprofit sector accountable. Our track record shows that unlike them, we don't just promise pie in the sky, we deliver."

Although their vision of peace, justice, and biodiversity may seem far-fetched and "un-American" in a culture of profit and plunder, these activists see their pie-throwing in line with the venerable tradition of political pranking. As journalist Jim Hightower asserts, "The BBB's pies are the Boston Tea Party of our modern day, sending a serious message softly to the corporate oligarchy."

Although the pie may be aimed symbolically at a particular *group* or *institution*, repercussions for political pie-throwing seem to vary according to the sense of humor of the *individual* targeted. Sometimes activists are able to "get away with it" since it is "all in jest." However, sometimes the target responds with the utmost humorlessness. The three activists who pied San Francisco Mayor Willie Brown in 1998, for example, were charged with felonies for conspiracy and battery. Dubbed the "Cherry Pie 3," they were convicted and sentenced to six months in prison. For their part, these pie-throwers never intended to hurt anyone; nevertheless, the prosecutors treated their act as a vicious attack on the mayor.

Of course, as Bakhtin observes, those in power rarely laugh. "The serious aspects of class culture are official and authoritarian. They are combined with violence, prohibitions, limitations, and always contain an element of fear and intimidation. Laughter, on the contrary, overcomes fear, for it knows no inhibitions, no limitations. Its idiom is never used by violence and authority." However, the vitriolic response of the state to a practical joke demonstrates the extremity and the ridiculousness of those in power.

Activists often assert that while the state attempts to prosecute them for the so-called violent act of pie-throwing, the state, along with its corporate cronies, commits acts of violence on a daily basis: evicting poor people, police brutality, clearcutting, polluting, bioengineering, warfare, and on and on.

"Speaking Pie to Power:" Post-Prank Discourse

As in almost all political actions, the press and its "telling" of the joke plays a key role in the pie prank. Like other forms of political performance, pranks are directed at a specific "victim" or target but also at a broader audience. According to folklorist Barre Toelken, pranks have several audiences: insiders who perform the trick, strangers who know little or nothing, and bystanders who are initiated, thereby becoming insiders themselves. Toelken points to the importance of these audiences as they strengthen the "esoteric sense of heightened participation in a special group." In other words, the performance of the prank solidifies the insider's identity and group cohesion. For some outsiders, the  prank can inform, educate, or convince; for others, of course, the prank can only embarrass, repulse, or ridicule.

The pie-throwers' communiqués and press releases contain other types of prankish language. The authors frequently *détourne* famous quotations and well-known proverbs, incorporating words and phrases associated with baking and pie. This use of humorous language is an additional wordplay, one that draws on well-known revolutionary rhetoric to heighten the practical joke of pie-throwing. The use of humor in both narrative and performance makes the BBB communiqués as deliciously mischievous as the pies themselves.

Humor can be a valuable political tool. As Saul Alinsky asserted in his activist handbook *Rules for Radicals*, "Ridicule is [hu]man's most potent weapon. It is almost impossible to counter-attack ridicule. It also infuriates the opposition, who then react to your advantage." For Bakhtin, comedy is related to the truth of the people: "This is why laughter could never become an instrument to oppress and blind the people. It always remained a free weapon in their hands." Pie-throwing utilizes this type of carnival humor, unsettling the authority and control that those in power try to project. While the pie-in-the-face is an act of mocking and derision, much like Bakhtin's notion of the carnivalesque, it also contains an element of hope and regeneration.

Audrey Vanderford writes about the performance of political protest in radical environmental and anarchist movements and has published articles on anarcha-feminism, pie-throwing, treesitting, and street theater. She resides in Eugene, Oregon, where she tries to balance family, activism, and graduate school. Check out Audrey's articles and a good collection of online anarchist resources at darkwing.uoregon.edu/~audreylv.

The Three Stooges: Class War Heroes?

BY RICHARD VON BUSACK, *METRO SANTA CRUZ*

The Three Stooges best era, roughly 1932 to 1950, coincides with some of the most troubled years in US history. By the 1950's the Stooges were prosperous, well-fed suburbanites, and it was a coasting decade for Moe and his partners. But they were at their finest impersonating near-homeless tramps dealing with the terrible Depression.

Don Morlan, a professor in communications at the University of Dayton, describes himself as "a lifelong Stooges fan" and a member of the Popular Culture Association, which holds annual conventions where Morlan and fellow academics discuss aspects of the Stooges' work.

A college professor who defends the Stooges is a novelty. Morlan once delivered a paper at the Conference on Popular Culture entitled "A Pie in the Face: The Three Stooges' Anti-Aristocracy Theme in Depression Era Film," which focused on "the ideological statements about economic class differences" in the Stooges' work.

"In seven or eight film shorts during the Depression," Morlan says, "the Stooges subject was bringing the aristocracy down to their own level, as in other pie fight comedies of the era."

The Stooges were not just pie fighters—they used that particular gag in only about 10 of their comedies. Morlan counts 34 out of 190 Stooges shorts as being about class conflict. He wrote in his paper, "Feature-length films in the 1930s that addressed Depression or financial class issues tended to ridicule the values of the rich rather than the people themselves. The Stooges did both." The Three Stooges wanted to wreck their own party, as in the 1936 film short *Ants in the Pantry* where they play exterminator-provocateurs. The trio attacked a mansion, salting the place with moths and mice to drum up business for their pest control service. We see a close-up of a tea-party cake being peppered with live ants.

The Stooges' shorts are often about work, always a touchy subject in the movies. Typically, Moe leads the troupe into a situation where they are highly unqualified. By the end, the machinery is in wreckage, and the Stooges have fled the scene. The usual setup finds them as door-to-door salesmen, mechanics or plumbers (as in their symphony of disaster, the 1940 film short *A Plumbing We Will Go*).

"The theme in these shorts," says Morlan, "is to bring the rich down to their level and shake their heads." Morlan is referring to the Stooges' fine

short *Hoi Polloi*, in which three bearded professors try—hopelessly—to give Moe, Larry and Curly the Eliza Doolittle treatment. A typical Stooges joke: When someone addressed them as "gentlemen," they would look over their shoulders to see who was meant.

There have been dozens of deeper or more subtle comedians in the century-long history of the movies, but have there ever been any that were more working-class than the Three Stooges?

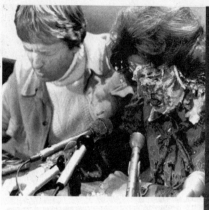

Agents
of
Pie-Kill Unlimited

BY JAMES JOHN BELL

"A SOCIETY CAN TOLERATE LESS AND LESS RANDOMNESS AS IT GROWS
EVER MORE ORDERED."
—ROBERT CHING, CHIEF AGENT, BROTHERHOOD OF ASSASSINS

The hot streets of night-time Miami swelled with protesters who were denied the ability to camp in the city's parks. Tom Forcade, founder of the Underground Press Syndicate, was outraged. He was one of many anti-war activists that Summer in Miami organizing direct actions, but his actions weren't all about controlling the streets. Forcade advocated utilizing spontaneity and chaos to confront power in the symbolic arena. Unlike the communists and socialists, his theories of revolution didn't come out of some guerrilla manifesto. They came from *Agent of Chaos*—a science fiction paperback that he carried around in his back pocket.

No, this isn't the 2003 battle in Miami to shut down the Free Trade Area of the Americas ministerial summit. Maybe Karl Marx was right, "History repeats. First as tragedy, then as farce." This battle in Miami took place during the Summer 1972 where both the Democratic and Republican National Conventions were being held. Forcade's Underground Press Syndicate was a lot like today's Independent Media Centers, albeit without the Internet. The protesters that got overrun in the streets, then and now, still haven't learned to expand their definition of protest into one that prioritizes contesting power in the broader symbolic, cultural, and ideological arenas rather than compete with militarized riot police for control of the street. A closer look at that old paperback in Forcade's pocket might help us understand why this continues to be the case.

Summer 1972 in Miami saw the rise of the Zippies—a revolutionary street army of Hippie Anarchists for the Miami Anti-Nixon Republican National Convention. It was a somewhat incoherent revolution (which was the point), with activists such as Abbie Hoffman and Forcade preaching that only true randomness can defeat the establishment and with the Zippies encouraging spontaneous acts of revolution. It was no surprise that activist Pat Small tossed a pie into the face of Councilman Harold Rosen of Miami Beach for not allowing the anti-war protesters a place to camp. In the meantime, Underground Press Syndicate Zip-pie organizers Rex Weiner and Deanne Stillman cooked up a plan that *Time* would call "the biggest fad since streaking." They organized a group of 10 people into the Agents of Pie-Kill Unlimited.

The idea for Pie-Kill was that people could hire an agent to pie their friends or enemies. Pie-Kill did birthday parties, weddings, bosses, landlords— you name it. The infamous Pieman relates one story where he "was hired by two 16-year-old girls who attended a Catholic parochial school to pie their principal, a 59-year-old crabby nun." More famous targets included New York City Mayor Abraham Beame, William Buckley, Nixon bagman Tony

Ulasewicz, pro-nuker Edward Teller, anti-feminist Phyllis Schlafly, Gordon Liddy, CIA Director William Colby, and even Andy Warhol.

"During the course of a couple of years, we threw about 600 pies and made lots of dough," remarks Weiner. He also points to *Agent of Chaos* by Norman Spinrad as his inspiration. "I gave myself the title of 'Chief Agent' (taking it right out of Spinrad's novel) and soon we were doing terrific business. What moved me to become Chief Agent of Pie-Kill Unlimited was the idea that emerges from the book that something as silly as a pie in the face can be more effective against rigid authority than a dozen protest marches. The key element is surprise."

Agent of Chaos is set four centuries into the future where the human race has expanded out into the entire solar system. Everyone is a Ward working for the Hegemony of Sol, which is ruled by the 10-man Hegemonic Council. There is no "democracy," instead the system of government is called "Order" and translates into total surveillance as well as the loss of personal freedoms in order to maintain peace and prosperity. Two political movements threaten the Hegemony—a band of rebels who fight for "democracy," the Democratic League, and the secretive and very chaotic Brotherhood of Assassins.

The Democratic League resorts to sabotage and guerrilla tactics in its fight to overthrow the Hegemony, but the League's actions become so predictable that the Hegemony keeps it around as an easily manipulated political scapegoat. The Hegemony, however, is deathly afraid of the Brotherhood of Assassins whose chaotic random acts seem mad and manage to constantly disrupt total authority. The Brotherhood takes as its inspiration an ancient sociological text written by the long dead Gregor Markowitz called "The Theory of Social Entropy."

The story of *Agent of Chaos* presents many parallels to revolutionary struggle that did not go unnoticed when the book was first published in 1967. During the late '60s and early '70s, anarchists likened themselves as the Brotherhood, saw do-gooder reformers as the League, and the authorities as the Hegemony. Forcade explained that the Zippies and Pie-Kill were like the Brotherhood, that the peace movement was the predictable League, and the establishment was the Hegemony.

"This means that there is a power structure (the Ins) and some people who are against it (the Outs)," explains Weiner while paraphrasing the strategic insights that he picked up from the book. Like Forcade, Weiner thought of the Ins as the establishment and the Outs as the peace movement. "The Outs must create their own power structure to be organized enough to fight the Ins. Both the Ins and the Outs become mirror images of each other because both are fighting against a mutual enemy: entropy, the tendency for things to fall apart. This is the reason why revolutions so often fail, why revolutionaries so quickly assume the character of their predecessors once they're in power." Pie-Kill was allied with no side, even Forcade got pied. Pie-Kill, like the Brotherhood in Spinrad's novel, was allied only with the force of chaos—entropy.

Spinrad's fictional Markowitz explains the theory of chaos as a strategy for revolution throughout the pages of *Agent of Chaos.* "It is wise," writes Markowitz,

"upon occasion to introduce true randomness into your actions when opposing an existing order. The servant of Order strives to force his enemy to accept the unacceptable. To serve Chaos, confront your enemy with the unacceptable—and he will eagerly choose any lesser evil you desire to make unavoidable." This chaotic interplay can be seen at work in movements like the Earth Liberation Front where property sabotage tactics usually force opponents into seeing other groups' tactics and demands as "more reasonable," such as Earth First!'s no compromise in defense of Mother Earth stance.

The tragic failure of today's mainstream reformer groups to install significant change in the power structure is paralleled in the novel by the Democratic League's failure to overthrow the Hegemony. "The League had merely been against something; there was nothing that it had been for. Even 'democracy' had been thought of as only the absence of the Hegemony—the negation of a negative, not a positive vision in its own right." The Brotherhood's Chief Agent Ching elaborates further on the futility of the League's strategy of revolutionary change: "The approach of your Democratic League was to fight that Order in an ordered manner. Since the Hegemony is far more ordered than the League could ever be, you could never obtain the social energy needed to substitute your Order for the existing Order. In fact, the League, as the 'disloyal opposition' absorbed much of the random hostility to the Hegemony and converted these random factors to predictable ones and thus actually contributed to the Order of the Hegemony."

Weiner puts the chaotic strategy of Ching's Brotherhood in Pie-Kill terms, "A simple, gooey cream pie, carefully thrown at precisely the wrong time (which is really the right time) in the face of the wrong person (who is actually the right person) can change history."

James John Bell is the editor of LastWizards.com and the co-founder of the strategic communication network smartMeme.com. If you like his science fiction perspectives on revolution, check out his afterword to John Brunner's The Sheep Look Up.

Menstrual Pies!

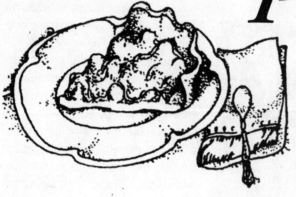

In 2003, Iain McIntyre interviewed Jessica Harrison on Australian Community Radio 3CR about the 1978 pieing of Mary Whitehouse.

Iain McIntyre: *For those who have now thankfully forgotten her, who was Mary Whitehouse?*

Jessica Harrison: She was the 1970s forerunner for much of the Christian fundamentalism that was to follow. Whitehouse was based in Britain where she was the core of a right-wing "family values" push. She and her followers would campaign for increased censorship of television, in the media, and generally against what was known then as the "permissive society." Behind her demure, little old lady image, she was very much against abortion and any kind of rights for women.

IM: What was she doing in Brisbane?

JH: She was on a national speaking tour. Given that the state of Queensland was incredibly conservative in the 1970s, she probably thought that she would be very popular there.

IM: Conventional protest tactics were quite difficult to use in Brisbane at that time weren't they?

JH: People forget now, but back in the late 1970s, there was a general ban on street marches and public protests in Queensland. Supposedly you could apply for a permit to protest, but the authorities would never give you one. Whenever people just went ahead and held a demonstration anyway, the police would come in and beat everyone up. They were extremely keen on stifling any form of public dissent. In fact, it was so repressive that one time when some friends and I were just zooming around having fun in the back of a flatbed truck, we were threatened with arrest for laughing too much!

IM: So did this influence your decision to use a pie?

JH: We were always looking for ways around these laws. At one point, we formed a religious sect devoted to the "Holy God of the Bank-book," which gave out weird and political tracts in shopping malls. On another occasion, we rode around on bikes with protest placards on our backs. In this case, we were inspired by what we had read about Aron Kay's spectacular pieing actions.

IM: What kind of recipe was involved?

JH: It was meant to be a menstrual blood pie, though no one was willing to donate at that time! So we had to use cochineal in an attempt to make it bright red, but the dye made it purple. Flavor-wise it was pretty soapy as we used what we regarded as a traditional recipe for shaving cream.

IM: How did it go down on the day?

JH: Once prepared, we all dressed up in our finest and entered as members of the public. One woman was actually a mother, but since she was quite small, she dressed up in a school uniform. Another of our members, a tall young guy, dressed in a suit to do the deed.

I remember feeling very uncomfortable wearing a dress, but I was also excited. In some ways, we were pretty scared since there weren't many of us—luckily Whitehouse's supporters didn't get violent.

When Whitehouse made her appearance, our friend let fly with the pie. Sadly, it didn't hit her right in the face, but it went all over her chest. A number of male voices immediately rang out in incredulous outrage that we could do such a disrespectful thing. She was totally flabbergasted, yet managed to make the comment that at least the pie matched the color of her dress.

We all rushed to the front to support the pie thrower but were hustled out quickly. A few people were arrested, but they were let off as often tends to happen in these situations. Basically, no one wanted to have to fly Whitehouse back from Britain to appear as a star witness.

IM: What was the reaction of the media?

JH: It got into all the newspapers. I remember seeing a photo of Whitehouse with pie running down her dress just after it happened. We weren't really doing it for media coverage, however, we just wanted to make her feel unwelcome. I guess we succeeded.

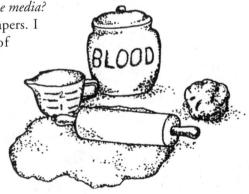

CREAM AND PUNISHMENT

Behind the Pies of Georges Le Gloupier

BY ROBERT CHALMERS
FROM *THE OBSERVER* MAGAZINE

"Permit me to recommend the bomb threat," Noël Godin said, pouring China tea from a delicate pot. "One little phone call, and it never fails. There are," he went on, "a thousand forms of subversion, all of them interesting. But few, in my opinion, can equal the convenience and immediacy of the cream pie."

A passerby, glancing through the window of Godin's living room, might take him for a tutor explaining some arcane point of literary history. Every room of his house in Brussels is lined with books and the whole place is kept in the kind of amiable disorder associated with the academic. After a few minutes, I noticed that our conversation was punctuated by a feeble mewing. A few feet away, huddled between the complete works of Jules Verne and a sheet of hardboard, a family of kittens had just been born.

On the table in front of Godin was a first edition of his 800-page *Anthology of Radical Subversion*; behind him, an immense picture of British film comedian Norman Wisdom. Both are items deeply cherished by Godin, a man of principle who likes to have fun. He arrived late and disheveled for our lunchtime appointment, straight off the morning express from Paris, weak from partying. The night before, he explained, he had missed the last train back, adjourned to "a number of nightclubs in the Bastille area," and had not been to bed.

Though he may look capable of no more aberrant an act than the drilling of irregular verbs at a minor public school, the author and provocateur is widely feared in France and Belgium where, under the pseudonym of "Georges Le Gloupier," he has taken to assaulting prestigious thinkers, media figures, and politicians with cream cakes. When Godin speaks, hardly a minute passes without the use of the verb entarter, which roughly translates as "to flan." "During the past 20 years," he boasts in the introduction to his recent autobiography, *Cream and Punishment*, "Le Gloupier has sent the best outfits of France's self-styled intellectuals to the dry cleaners."

Recipients have included Jean-Luc Godard, the film director, and Marguerite Duras, the novelist. In VIP lounges at the Cannes Film Festival, what Godin calls "cream psychosis" has become so widespread that even Gérard Depardieu is reported to have developed a preference for hotels' rear entrances. At the 1997 festival, victims included the new French minister of culture, who is unlikely to forget his first public engagement, and the philosopher Bernard-Henri Levy, hit for the fifth time.

Godin showed me a video of this last operation, which shows Levy—as famous for his chest hair, silk blousons, and Christian Dior shirts as for his philosophy—arriving at the Nice airport with his third wife, actress Arielle Dombasle. As they checked in, shadowy figures could be seen in the background, ladling cream.

"They pick up their boarding cards, as you can see," said Godin, who has clearly watched this shaky footage hundreds of times but, like a footballer reviewing the goal of his career, seems unlikely to tire of it. "Then three entarteurs fall on them, with me leading the charge. They shout: 'Oh no. Oh not again.' I deliver my cake, and Levy responds with punches. One of my young female comrades flans him again, point blank, while a second woman crushes a layered chocolate gateau topped with creme chantilly over the head of Arielle Dombasle. It was at that point," Godin added, "that things got out of hand."

Godin's recent operations have been heavily covered in mainstream periodicals, and even the most responsibly minded publications have reported his unusual campaign sympathetically. When he arrived at Cannes last month, Godin recalled: "I was greeted with cheerful cries of 'Bonjour Monsieur L'Entarteur,' 'Who is it this year?,' and 'Give my regards to Bernard-Henri Levy'." His surprising popularity, Godin says, is the result of his careful vetting of targets, who tend to be figures with a limited sense of irony at their own expense. "I flan people with the aim to denounce them in some way. I do not want to slide into facile sensationalism. Every victim has to be thoroughly justified."

Few have been more outstanding flanees that Levy, a man so sensitive that he was once credibly reported as observing that "when I find a new shade of gray, I feel ecstatic." Levy has also famously remarked that he dislikes seeing a woman pay in a restaurant. "I think," Levy explained, "that money does not suit a woman; or rather that I would not fall in love with such a woman." His own varied talents constitute, by his own account, "a landscape that does not have a fixed place in the classic topography of culture."

These are the kinds of observations that guarantee the philosopher express deliveries of creme chantilly for years to come. "He is the worst," says Godin, who, on the subject of Levy, tends to sound like Herbert Lom on Inspector Clouseau. Godin has been especially critical of Levy's consistent urging of armed intervention against the Bosnian Serbs, given that the philosopher, unlike other intellectual militants such as André Malraux or George Orwell, has shown no inclination to enlist himself.

But if a taste for personal involvement has not been a feature of Levy's contribution to the Bosnia debate, he cannot be accused of having shrunk from unarmed combat once the pies started flying. At Levy's baptismal flanning, in Liege 10 years ago, the author of *Testament of God* delivered an unambiguous response. "I didn't even feel the uppercut," Godin told me, "because I was so happy to gaze up from the floor and see the peak of French intellectual thought so thoroughly snowbound."

Levy, who emerges from his books as a reflective man unshakably committed to qualities such as reasonableness and tolerance, was dismayed to find that footage of the incident—which shows him shouting to his prone assailant: "Get up or I'll kick your head in"—was repeatedly broadcast on French television.

On their second encounter, at a Brussels bookshop where a gathering of what Godin describes as "100 painted old trout" had come to hear the thinker read from his work *The Last Days of Baudelaire*, Godin was laid out on a table and subjected to further blows. The film of their latest incident, which shows Dombasle scratching and lashing out at the entarteur's woman companions, ends with an abrupt thump. "Levy broke the camera," says Godin, "then punched the cameraman on the nose. A few minutes later he had his hands around my neck while Arielle Dombasle thrashed at me with her handbag. The police got me out of there."

Such episodes have done little to enhance Levy's profile. In Japan, Godin claims, footage of the French philosopher's viscous misfortune has proved so popular with game-show viewers that Godin is known as "a kind of Belgian Jerry Lewis." "Levy was flanned in Reims by a mysterious splinter group," said Godin, "and recently I heard that he also ran into difficulties in a bakery at Montpellier. If those reports are true, he is under fire from all sides."

The first five seconds after the delivery of a flan, Godin believes, offer a stark revelation of a victim's real character. Jean-Luc Godard, for instance, accepted his projectile with good grace and later intervened to stop his assailant from being banned for life from the Cannes festival. "Accurately delivered, a cream pie is an uncannily precise barometer of human nature," Godin argued. "If Levy, for example, could once respond with humor or self-deprecation, he would immediately defuse the process and turn the whole business in his favor."

The phone rang. Godin answered it, then started to speak in a series of code words. "Geneva," he explained to me, conspiratorially. "An operation."

Godin earns a living as an author and a cinema historian, but he also makes an occasional appearance as an actor. His brief appearance in the role of the Belgian writer Pierre Mertens is the highlight of the otherwise uneven film *The Sexual Life of the Belgians*, directed by his friend Jan Bucquoy.

Increasingly, however, Godin's time is given over to les tartes. Attacks are meticulously planned and require a minimum of four people, including a camera operator, a stills photographer, and an assistant to hold the pastry. "The crucial thing is not to throw the flan, but place it and, most importantly, not to give a damn about finding a safe escape route, even if that means being beaten senseless by dreary security guards. We only use the finest patisserie," he added, "ordered at the last minute from small local bakers. Quality is everything. If things go wrong, we eat them."

Sometimes, Godin told me, his team can be 18 strong, with several members dressed in the official costume of Georges Le Gloupier: a preposterous outfit consisting of a false beard, reading glasses, and a bow tie. Entarteurs are strictly forbidden from responding physically to attacks, however violent. As of yet, none of his victims have pressed charges. "They would love to," Godin said, "but it would be disastrous for what they hold most dear—their public reputation. When I have been detained in custody, my arresting officers have usually been weak with laughter, and several have offered me their own list of future candidates."

The history of the flans is a bizarre and perverse one. Born and educated in Liege, Godin abandoned his law studies when he got caught up in the student demonstrations of May 1968. The following year, fired with enthusiasm for the anarchist principles he has never forsaken, he was hired to write the news column for *Friends of Film*, a magazine published by the Belgian Catholic League.

"I started to print complete falsehoods—gradually at first, then routinely," he recalled. "I invented non-existent films that I illustrated with snapshots of my relatives. I wrote face-to-face interviews with hundreds of artists, including Frank Capra and Robert Mitchum, without ever leaving my bedroom."

Readers of *Friends of Film* were introduced to the work of imaginary geniuses such as Sergio Rossi, Aristide Beck, and Viviane Pei, the Thai director of such films as *The Lotus Flower Will No Longer Grow on the Shores of Your Island*. Pei's achievements, ceaselessly lauded in Godin's column, were the more remarkable, he reported, in that she was "the only blind director in the history of cinema." He enthused over *Vegetables of Good Will*, in which Claudia Cardinale played an endive, and *Germinal II*, a Maoist cartoon featuring Jean-Louis Barrault as the voice of a cold chisel.

When I voiced my skepticism, Godin produced a complete run of the magazine, carefully preserved in chronological order and clearly authentic. In the first column I saw, Jeanne Moreau revealed Roger Vadim, former husband of Brigette Bardot, to be "a do-it-yourself fanatic secretly obsessed with small balsawood aircraft." Elsewhere, subscribers to *Friends of Film* learnt that Marlene Dietrich led expeditions to hunt down the Loch Ness monster, that Michael Caine had a motor that ran on yogurt, and that Marcel Pagnol had crossed the English Channel on a four-poster bed fitted with an outboard motor.

Godin's interest in flans began when he wrote a report stating that one of his fictional characters, Georges Le Gloupier, had assaulted director Robert Bresson with a cream pie. In the next issue, he alleged that Marguerite Duras, a friend of Bresson, had launched a revenge attack on Le Gloupier with a kirsch gateau at a café in Saint-Germain-des-Pres.

"A few days later," Godin continued, "I heard that Duras was really coming to Belgium. With the help of a few Oud Zottegem—our explosive bedside beer—the plan was hatched." Godin attended the function and pressed a large cream cake into Duras' face as she elucidated the theme of her second film, *Destroy, She Says*. In the next issue of *Friends of Film*, he reported the incident as a revenge attack by Le Gloupier.

Before I met Godin, I had expected his activities to be some kind of contrived form of performance art. Little could be further from the truth. A kind of earnest joy radiates from him when he talks about what he calls his "cream crusade." He sometimes raises his hand to his mouth, like a child, in a vain attempt to stop himself from smiling at the pleasure of it. While most of the volumes in his vast library are formidable-looking anarchist texts, a high percentage of his 10,000 videos are slapstick films. He owns the complete works of the Three Stooges and Will Hay and—worryingly, for a man who speaks no English—14 films by George Formby. When that first *tarte a la creme* was launched, you feel, his disparate interests instantly cohered. Suddenly, it all made sense.

As a young man, Godin disseminated tracts urging workers to engage in minor acts of sabotage. "A match jammed in a Yale lock," he suggested. "An error in the accounts, a bomb threat, a drop of tar in a surveillance camera."

His principles have barely altered. Godin has lived with his girlfriend Sylvie for 17 years, but he remains opposed to the institution of family and will not have children "because it would be irresponsible to bring them into this tragic world."

His genial, bookish demeanor and mischievous good humor somehow allows him to sound endearingly innocent even when pleading the most controversial of causes. "I cannot help admiring irregular combatants," Godin told me. "I have a powerful sympathy for the Baader gang, for instance. They gambled their lives, and it was an adventure that could only end one way. Their commitment reminds me of the flame that burns in the novels of Dumas or the films of Howard Hawks: unbridled friendship, reckless *joie de vivre*, the love of risk, the refusal to accept any limits."

Few could accuse Godin of less than total commitment to his own surreal struggle against self-importance and conformity. Take his own career as a director, which produced bizarre film shorts. His second film, *Trump Trump Trala*, is the story of a woman suddenly seized with the desire to revolt against her oppressed condition. "To sum up," says Godin, "she fires on soldiers with a catapult, flans repressive parents, flagellates bailiffs, urinates in the street, blows up police stations, and incites the pillage of the supermarket Monoprix." To his surprise, Godin won a national competition for Best Short Film.

"I had a dilemma there," he recalled. "The award was presented by a mayor—the personification of every value I found most distasteful. But the prize was two movie cameras. In the end, I went up to the podium and threw my arms round him. I said: 'Thank you, thank you, thank you my mayor.' I kissed and licked him all over. I pushed him over and with our limbs intertwined, we rolled around on the stage while I covered him with kisses. This went on for quite a while. 'Thank you, my mayor, thank you.' Every time he tried to get up, I hauled him back by the buttocks."

You could hardly accuse Godin of having mellowed with age. Far from fading away as its novelty wears off, Godin's campaign appears to be gathering momentum. He is in regular contact with groups in Paris, Canada, and Switzerland, where five cabinet ministers were recently entarted.

Did Godin and his co-conspirators not consider that they had already made their point? "On the contrary," he said, "we are just beginning. We feel ready now. Ready to attack another sort of target. A genuine International Patisserie Brigade has been born. We believe that we are capable of achieving great things in the near future. For instance," he went on, "I firmly believe that we can flan the Pope. We were waiting for him on May 13, 1994, in Brussels with some delicately flavored surprises, but as you know, he providentially slipped on a bar of soap."

"Sylvie is worried that I might end up getting shot," said Godin. "Personally, I have considerable faith in the professionalism of elite bodyguards, who are, on the whole, reasonably alert. Alert enough, that is, to recognize a cream cake if they have had advance warning about it. But that is a risk that will not enter into our calculations for one moment. So great is the ardor that has seized us— not just me, but the basic combat group—that we will go all the way."

Godin's interest in new and more prestigious victims must, I supposed, have taken the heat off his old enemy Levy. "Sadly not," said Godin. "I offered my terms for a ceasefire several months ago. Hostilities will end when he and his wife appear in public and sing, as a duet, the popular French comic song *"Avez-Vous Vu Le Beau Chapeau De Zozo?"* So far he has shown no sign of complying. Consequently Levy's astrologers, if they are to be trusted, will have been warning of a high-calorie disaster that awaits him at the beginning of next year. This is something of a break with tradition; he is accustomed to having a year's respite between helpings."

On a recent operation involving Levy, Godin claims, the cream pies were carried through a security barrier strapped to Alfred, a performing dog. "Alfred is a pedigree," said Godin, "but I refuse to reveal the breed. I like the thought of Levy experiencing a feeling of slight unease every time he sees a dog at a public function."

A keen Anglophile, Godin says he is planning to visit London, in a professional capacity. "I would like to appeal to like-minded people in the United Kingdom," Godin said. "Invite me over. Propose a plan of action." He opened the small notebook that contains his hit lists and showed me the beginnings of his British section. Godin says he is already investigating the movements of two other figures from what he considers to be an abundant supply of potential British targets. "The escalation in the international flan war," he told me, "has already begun. No obstacle can stand in our way. Like Errol Flynn, Clark Gable, Gene Tierney, and Barbara Stanwyck in the old Hollywood films, we have a crazed belief in ourselves. We pose a direct threat to everything that is most pompous, from Margaret Thatcher to the Pope."

Godin hopes to be over "to brighten the lives of my British friends" some time toward the end of the year. Could he be more precise? "Tell them to expect me," he said, "when they see a cream-colored shooting star traverse their cheerless skies."

The History of the BBB

from the Earth First! Journal 20th Anniversary Special Edition

Little is known about the true origins of the BBB. Some say it grew out of the Whiskey Rebellion in the late 1700s in Pennsylvania; others say it began in a feud between two bakeries in Paris during the mid-1800s. However, after much painstaking research, our agents have uncovered the first known account of the pastry uprising, set during the Habsburg Dynasty in Spain, mid-1600s. Philip IV, who succeeded to the throne in 1621, preferred culture to politics and allowed Gaspar de Guzman Conde de Olivares to run the government. Olivares' efforts to increase taxation and conscription led to revolt in 1640, first in Catalonia and then in Portugal.

A small group of bakers were fed up with Olivares and formed an underground resistance group called La Brigada Biotic de la Hornada. They plotted an attack on Olivares, and in a show of solidarity with Portugal and Catalonia, they made their move late one evening when he was entertaining the Prince of Austria, another member of the Habsburg Dynasty. The bakers posed as royal chefs, and just as dinner was being served, they delivered him his just desserts. The agent yelled *"¡Dé Portugal de nuevo a la gente!"* ("Give Portugal back to the people!"), as she hurled the pie directly into Olivares' face.

Since this action, numerous pies have been tossed in many deserving faces around the world. What follows is an account of the BBB's modern development within the North American Earth First! movement. The story begins with a mud-slinging contest in the hallowed pages of the *EF! Journal* after a few folks said that they would have pied Ed Abbey had the chance arisen because of his racist comments about turning Mexican immigrants back at the US border.

Subject: Dear Shit fer Brains... May 1, 1989
Dear Comrades,
Amidst the mourning and merry-waking [sic], we make this warning: The Biotic Baking Brigade of ¡Mirth First! first formed with the intention, among others, of delivering a lovely refried-bean pie unto the venerated visage of the late lamented author [Ed Abbey]. However, he has since slipped our slapstick and is beyond the range of even more accurate pie-flingers than the Relentless Fanatic. Heaven and Hell alike may turn him back at the border, but the Earth will digest him as it does all. The frijole torte remains. It waits for the face of bigotry and fascism to show itself again, or for the crassest [sic] eulogist

to the "anarchist" who loved borders. Nopale Ed knows no limits now. Neither do we. Simply,
—Simon "Chico" Zapotes and BBB, ¡Mirth First!

Subject: Dear Shit fer Brains... June 21, 1989
Dear Cranial Feces,
To paraphrase Merle Haggard, "If you're runnin' down Ed Abbey, man, you're walkin' on the fightin' side of me." I direct this comment to "Simon 'Chico' Zapotes and BBB, ¡Mirth First!" Your letter last *Journal* crossed the line. Ed Abbey was my friend and a great man. I'm honored to have known him and am angered by those pretentious juvenile ideologues who insult his name. Come forth! Identify yourselves, you cowardly scum, and take responsibility for the slime that leaks from your ideologically enslaved brains to your slovenly pens.
I hope to meet you in some dark lonely place. Soon.
For the Earth First!,
—Howie Wolke, Darby, Montana

Subject: Dear Shit fer Brains... September 22, 1989
Dear EF! & Howie,
In response to your letter in the last *Journal*, the Revolutionary Ecoterrorist Pie Brigade (REPB) has this to say: To set the record straight, we are in no way affiliated with the Biocentric Baker's Brigade! (BBB) [sic]. We purged that faction for their deviationist ideology, revisionist interpretations of the Unassailable Doctrines, and for their vanguardist tendencies. They engage in petty boulangerie hooliganism for the furtherance of their hidden agenda and are usurpers! They dared to mock Betty-Crocker-Thought with their infantile propaganda! We have nothing to do with such counter-revolutionary decadence. We, the REPB, are the leading proponents of culinary terrorism and have mastered the science of Pastry Revolution. We are preparing to lead the masses on to Global Ecological Paradise using their Historically Available Instrument of eco-meringue and pretentious ideology. We have the correct line on The-Way-It-Is and anyone who is offended by this letter deserves to be!
—Chairman Mikal, REPB
PS. No, Howie, I didn't write either the BBB or ¡Mirth First! letters if you might possibly be thinking that. However, it was Simon "Chico" Z., myself, and another who originated the idea of giving Abbey a frijole pie! And he would've loved it! Too bad we never got the chance. But, oh well, there are other deserving faces (if you know what I mean).

Subject: Dear Shit fer Brains... September 22, 1989

O Brave Beloved Biotic Compadres,

Suffer me speech a short span whilst I return the glove that one of our fellow EF! followers has foolishly flung at my feet. Howie Wolke of Darby, Montana, seems to have a beef about my last letter. Apparently, the late Prosaic Laureate of ecocentrism is a sacred cow, and Howie has moved into the ring to defend him while I remain in the shadows. I mistook him for a sacred clown. The value of sacred clowns, of mudhead kachinas in their mudpie kitchens, is that by ruthlessly criticizing everyone, they allow us finally, after the mud has settled, to embrace each other honestly and to know fully who we are. Especially because we are constantly challenging loggers and other industrial addicts to fundamentally change their lives, we should ourselves be willing to accept challenges to our fundamental behaviors, such as diet and relationships. Blind tolerance, such as some have preached, will only result in a false calm until our docility is disrupted by a panicked intolerance, and we are stampeded to slaughter. Sacred clowns try to wake the herd up before we get to the cliffs.

Why, then, do I remain outside the firelight? Anonymity is essential to sacred clowns, so the laughing stock responds not to them but to the issues. (My beckoning boxer is far beefier than I, and I doubt I would find his fighting side much prettier than his wit.) Moreover, I do not stalk prey in the open; I like to stay hidden on the edges. There are others here in the brush, and a good reason why many of us use different names is so They (the industrial steering committee) won't know quite who or how many we are. And when you've hunted yourself it makes sense to stay in the woods. Finally, I find the names I choose myself certainly as real as my legal, Christian name. I am an ambling mammal labeled numerous names. Amongst others, I remain truly,

—Simon "Coyote" Zapotes

PS. Howie: I'm not who you think, i.e. my initials have never been M.J., but I'll bet that when the pie hits, he and E.A. will be laughing together 'til the cows go home.

But since the mid-1600s in Iberia, no pies had yet been thrown under the name of the BBB until Judi Bari took Pie-rect Action...

In the Spring 1994, the BBB came into fruition through the inspiration of Judi Bari. The pie-ee was attorney Mark Goldowitz of Oakland, who represented some homeowners from the Albion, California, area who were being sued by Louisiana Pacific over a 54 day, 15 treesit 1992 mega-action called the "Albion Nation Uprising." Goldowitz claimed to be a SLAPP (Strategic Lawsuits Against Public Participation) suit specialist and was involved in the drafting of California's first anti-SLAPP law. Goldowitz sucked about $60,000 out of one activist's homeowner insurance policy for a few months work, but he was unsuccessful in getting anyone out of the SLAPP suit. Earth First!ers and Albion residents were pissed at him for being such a gold digger (they called him Mark Goldiggerwitz). If the other homeowner insurance companies had all been paying at the same rate, Goldowitz would have taken in more than $500,000 for less than six months work.

Judi had been long scheduled to do a panel on SLAPP suits at the Public Interest Environmental Law Conference in Eugene, Oregon. Goldowitz showed up and refused to take part in her panel, but he took copious notes during her presentation and then got himself scheduled at the last minute to do a separate presentation that afternoon at a time conflicting Judi's repeated panel. Her morning panel was lightly attended due to schedule conflicts with other popular activities and panels. Judi decided, most likely before the conference, that Goldowitz needed pastry therapy, but his arrogant behavior sealed his fate. Unfortunately, having been a bomb victim, Judi was unable to physically throw a pie with any amount of force herself (she had been a brown belt and extremely agile before the bombing). So Judi recruited there on the spot an instant member of the BBB. Together, they walked up to Goldiggerwitz in the hallway of the university and heaved a pie at him, gracing him with his just desserts.

Three years later the BBB struck again, flanning the CEO of Maxxam, Charles Hurwitz, who was busy chopping down redwoods to pay off junk bond debts. But it wasn't until Bill Gates was pied the next year in Belgium, and then Milton Friedman in San Francisco, that the planetary pastry resistance began to rise.

OPERATION DESSERT STORM

Tofu Cream Must Be as Global as Capital

Briefing from Agent Geek Sorbet

Revolution is about doing things out of the ordinary. I think about what it will be like everyday, and I expect to be shocked and surprised by any revolution. Pie-throwing embraces so many beautiful aspects of humanity, it's strange it doesn't happen everyday.

First of all, there's the great video footage. The look on the victim's face is unique, unreproducible in a script or on a set. Do they taste The Pie? Does the sweet flavor complicate their outrage? Most news presenters, and a nation lapping it up, are surprised and shocked. It is proclaimed as violent, although in a time when it was "entertainment," at the turn of the 20th century, similar acts of "propaganda by deed" were more likely to be bombs. Violent indeed.

Second, it is merely the act of a clown. That lovable self-abusive humor merchant. It's funny to watch. Despite your "outrage," deep down you see the humor, yeah? A little pie never hurt anybody. It follows in the tradition of the larrikin.

Third, it's pleasant to be again reminded that we are merely monkeys. We are all human, even the richest and most powerful. You could be forgiven for believing that these people are somehow untouchable, special, above, or separate from us.

The revolution in Chiapas against neoliberalism and globalization—the struggle for *tierra y libertad*—has influenced us profoundly. As Marcos and others have demonstrated so effectively, in today's world of ecological and social meltdown, we all live in Chiapas. But the Zapatistas have encouraged us to bring *Zapatismo* to our own communities, and we have done what we can to follow through on that. In other words: think globally, act locally... and when the likes of Monsanto's Shapiro and Novartis' Watson came to our home territories, we pied the polluting lollies.

The great moments of revolutionary history have all been enormous popular festivals—the storming of the Bastille, the uprisings of 1848, the Paris Commune, the revolutions of 1917-1919, Paris '68. Conversely, popular festivities have always been looked on by the authorities as a problem, whether they have banned, tolerated, or semi-institutionalized them. Why does power fear free celebration? Could it be something to do with the utopian urges that seize a crowd becoming aware of its own power? From the Middle Ages onward, the carnival has offered glimpses of the world turned upside down—a topsy-turvy universe free of toil, suffering, and inequality.

Carnival celebrates temporary liberation from the prevailing truth and the established order; it marks the suspension of hierarchical rank, privileges, norms, and prohibitions. Carnival is not a spectacle seen by the people; they live in it, and everyone participates because its very idea embraces all people.

Ultimately, it is in the streets that power must be dissolved. The streets are where daily life is endured, suffered, and eroded, and where power is confronted and fought, it must be turned into the domain where daily life is enjoyed, created, and nourished.

Call to Action to Purveyors of Sweet Humility Everywhere

OK, you've all heard the puns before so let's just cut to the base. The time is baked for the pie-throwing resurgence to rise together: Let's globalize the pie.

A global month of action: April Fool's Day until May Day 2001.

Tofu cream must be as global as capital.

Following on the fine tradition of the BBB and the many individuals who have inspired us all with pies in the faces of Bill Gates, Milton Freidman, Steve Bracks, et al., we call on you to partake in Operation Dessert Storm.

What better way to draw attention to the often faceless leaders of the corporate world, shameful "journalists," dodgy politicians, and anyone who deserves a face full of dissent.

The "global movement" is often misrepresented in the corporate media. You can't misrepresent a face full of cream. It sends a clear message to the recipient and to the media that what these people are doing is ridiculous and that you are prepared to let them know—and to have some fun while doing it!

The pie is the great equalizer. How many times have you wanted to see whipped cream smeared on John Howard's glasses or see Tony Blair choking on a strawberry? Now is your chance—mobilize en masse and pie!

LET THEM EAT CAKE

Why I Pied Dr. Neil First

BY DAVID PIKE
A.K.A. AGENT CREAMY GENES

I smooshed a whipped cream pie in the face of geneticist Neil First in March 1999, in order to humble a man arrogant enough to create living creatures from cold science. First is a top-level scientist involved in animal cloning and the general field of genetic engineering.

At the time, this field included such "wonders" as potatoes and corn that internally produce pesticides, thereby forcing us to consume the pesticide with the vegetable. Genetically engineered soybeans are resistant to herbicides, thereby increasing the use of poisonous chemicals on this food. A breakthrough dubbed "terminator technology" has created plants whose seeds turn out sterile and stop future generations. This insures profit for the seed companies. Many genetically altered plants are already in production in the US, and one estimate puts the chance of processed food products containing genetically altered ingredients at 30 percent.

In the area of animal research, attempts are being made to engineer pigs with human genes to make their meat more tender. Mice are being created with all sorts of variations for laboratory testing. And some scientists want to grow human organs for transplants.

I believe these efforts violate the basis of life on this planet: the DNA of organisms. Slicing and splicing the genetic code of life is inexcusable and to then patent or profit from this is criminal.

I see the geneticists of today as parallel with the Nazi doctors of the Third Reich. To them, the human race is the master race and the rest of life is disposable. Plants may be mutated and animals mutilated for any whim of human "need" or greed. Unwanted species may even be genetically eradicated or replaced with an "improved" version in the newest eugenics.

Faced with these nightmares, I decided to use humorous mischief to bring people's attention to the subject. Genetic engineering is spreading rapidly with barely any public education or consideration. Because I "assaulted" this madness and the ego of one of its perpetrators, I am identified as a resistant strain with several police departments dispatched to isolate me from society.

The cream-pie-in-the-face slapstick routine has been used many times in the past by politically motivated clowns on arrogant authority figures. The Yippies did it during the Vietnam War. And who doesn't remember the great pie fights in old black-and-white movies? The cream pie must be de-criminalized. Humor must replace fear.

Genetic engineering and cloning must stop.

The Pie-Rect Side of Eco-Activism
An Interview with Agent Pecan

FROM *THE TIMES* OF INDIA

The crusade for Ecotopia is spreading itself thick with the emergence of the BBB. The redoubtable BBB has exemplified underground eco-activism in recent years with its avowed goal of pie-rect action—attacking global capitalism full in the face with pie, preferably custard or cherry. Their "Tried and Pied" list of entartements includes technocrats, policy makers, heads of trade bodies, politicians, and corporate honchos.

But has the BBB brand of pielitical pressure paid off? In an exclusive interview in November 1999, a leader of the movement who gave his name as Agent Pecan minced no words on the group's mission. Excerpts are included here:

Times of India: How did the idea of pie-throwing originate?

Agent Pecan: In my consciousness, pie-throwing was something that was done in the movies to bring someone down off of their high horse. The pie had universal visual meaning. With an understanding of the Situationists' idea of disrupting the spectacle and using the disruption to point out the cracks in the official reality, the power of the pie was given whole new opportunities to cast light on shadowy figures. Tasteful entertainment at protest prices.

TOI: The splashy approach seems to be a trifle too hard on the egos of your beneficiaries. Is pie-throwing as soft as it looks, going by the media splash you have generated?

AP: Pieing is not so much a personal attack, as it is an attack on authority, secrecy, corruption, and greed. If the ego of the person pied is bruised, that is not the intent. But shame can be a powerful motivator, and it can persuade people to change their behavior. This, of course, is an unintended result, for the goal is to disrupt the spectacle and expose the lies official reality requires for its existence.

In my case, State Representative Carol Flynn, whom I pied, said the only thing that hurt was her self-esteem. No physical injury. A pastry projectile took her down a notch, and it exposed her violation of the law and her racist lies.

TOI: Isn't pie-throwing a legal offense, as in causing a public nuisance? Is operating underground the result of or the very backbone of the movement?

AP: Most pie-throwers try to escape and are underground. Some are caught.

I chose to stay and explain my actions, so I did not run. I had something to say, and I wanted to take it to trial to say it. I was convicted of a misdemeanor.

TOI: Given an option, to what other methods would you seek recourse in order to spread awareness?

AP: There are all kinds of methods to raise peoples' awareness. Pie is a particular tactic that is great in some circumstances, and in others, the results would not be

What do
you get for
the pie that has
everything?

A Target

quite as sweet. Pie injects humor into protest, and a visual esperanto, a universal message that is conveyed via action that everyone understands.

TOI: You prefer the electronic media for a slice of the action.

AP: The idea behind pie is to spin the spectacle so that the creators/keepers of the official reality must respond.

TOI: What about allegations that the gravity of eco-policy decisions are being drowned in splashes of pie?

AP: The media does damage control mostly by focusing on the pie and the pie-thrower, not on the actions of the target that led to the pieing. So, some may argue that the message was lost. In my case, it never came out in the media that Flynn admitted on the witness stand to violating the law, abusing the power of her office, and telling racist lies. But it did go out through the media that she refused to hear legislation pertaining to the issue (not quite accurate, but nearly so). The pie forced people to ask why someone would do such a thing, question the state's explanation, and it created tremendous visibility for our campaign, as well as recruitment opportunities to get more people involved. The specifics of the issue are covered in pastry puff and indiscernible with this type of action, but the issue in general is thrust into the face of the public.

TOI: How positive has the victim's approach been after the "treatment?" Do those who fling the pie expect to change hearts?

AP: Well, we never expect to create a change in the decision of the project when we pie, but we do intend to expose the corruption of the process in the pieing of the individual most directly linked to that corruption.

TOI: Do you hold faith in environmental summits?

AP: No.

TOI: How often have you participated in the proceedings and put forward workable proposals on environmental management?

AP: Very often. I, for one, have sat on governmental advisory boards, done electoral and issue politics for 10 years.

TOI: On your opposition to the neoliberal paradigm. What is the ideal balance of power you envision between corporates and governments in the coming century?

AP: The real question is do we even want to abdicate our power, community autonomy, and self-determination to nation states that represent the interests of the wealthy or to corporations that represent their interests? Neither. Not to corporations or governments. Mutual aid, and an end to consumer culture. Really going back way before agriculture. Primitivism. Take from the Earth what it offers, instead of changing the Earth to fit our preferences.

TOI: What is your vision of an eco-safe world?

AP: Civilization must end, and we must go feral. I just wanna be a naked monkey on a rock. We are animals, with no more or less right to live on this world than any other animal, plant, or rock.

The Life Cycle of a Pie

most pies are baked, then set to cool
upon a windowsill—
it gives them time to think a bit,
it gives them time to chill.

besides the oven, whence they came
they haven't any clue—
and what their purpose is in life
they haven't either—true.

now once upon a time, some say,
('twas almost like a dream!)
a pie sat on a windowsill
made out of tofu creme.

and what its destiny might be,
it pondered long and long—
never imagining its fame
in poem and story and song.

the pie was loaded in a box,
and taken out and flung—
hosannas in the highest!
the bells in steeples rung.

it ended life a cheerful smear
that dribbled down a face—
avenging Mother Nature
in the proper time and place.

a life is good (some people say)
when it is ended well—
few pies have had a better end—
and that is all i'll tell.

—Dennis Fritzinger
Poet Laureate of the Global Pastry Uprising

Pie-rect Action I: Scoundrels

"And here I end, having put my Arm as far as my strength will go to advance Righteousness: I have Writ, I have Acted, I have Pied, I have Peace: and now I must wait to see the Spirit do its own work in the hearts of others, and whether England shall be the first Land, or some others, wherein Truth shall sit down in triumph."
—THE DIGGER GERRARD WINSTANLEY (1650)

Milton Friedman and Fascist Economics

The BBB struck a blow against globalization when an operative threw a pie in the face of neoliberal economist Milton Friedman at a San Francisco conference Friedman had organized on the privatization of public education. The incident occurred on October 9, 1998, at approximately 6:30 p.m., immediately before

former Secretary of State (under President Reagan) George Schultz was to deliver the keynote address to the conference titled, "School Choice and Corporate America."

"When it comes to defending the Earth from the scum of the corporate universe, the pie's the limit!" proclaimed an agent of the BBB. He approached Friedman while the nobel laureate was glad-handing a crowd of supporters, said "Mr. Friedman, it's a good day to pie!," and flopped the tasty coconut creme pie in his face.

"We hold Milton Friedman responsible for crimes against the people by organizing this appalling conference, which calls for the privatization of public education. Friedman serves as the world's pre-eminent neoliberal economist, supporting globalization and 'free trade' policies that have brought the world poverty, misery, starvation, and ecological devastation. The global market has brought the globe to the brink of economic collapse.

photo by Warry

"As a young American, what can I look forward to under neoliberal economics besides a depressing McWorld? This cutthroat economic system has devastating impacts globally as well as in my own backyard. I have witnessed the abuse of fellow activists as they have been arrested, jailed, beaten, pepper-sprayed, and killed for trying to defend the Headwaters forest from fascist economics."

The Robert Shapiro Incident
A Strange and Terrible Saga
An Eyewitness Account

BY AGENT APPLE

On October 23, 1998, I was contacted by a BBB intelligence source known as "Deep Pastry." S/he communicated to me that Robert Shapiro, CEO and chairman of Monsanto, would be delivering a keynote address at a conference the following week in San Francisco. We had heard from Our Man in London recently that the Brits were planning to pie Shapiro the next time he crossed the Atlantic, and naturally we couldn't let the Limeys upstage us in this respect.

I immediately relayed the information to the General Command of the BBB, whose headquarters and ovens are located deep in the heart of the Headwaters redwood forest. The following day, I received my orders: compile a dossier on the target (photos, personal habits, culinary preferences, etc.), perform an extensive reconnaissance of the battlefield (the illustrious Fairmont Hotel, where Clinton and his ilk stay when they come to town), assemble a crack pie-slinging team, develop a set of combat scenarios, and await the go-ahead command.

When the day in question arrived, everything was in place. I went to the pre-arranged bake shop (name withheld for obvious reasons), ordered a apple-rhubarb crumble to go, and repaired to the pub. Even though I expected the document and have been through the routine before, I couldn't help but tremble a tad when I reached the bottom of the patisserie and uncovered the sealed, embossed envelope that read, "For Your Pies Only." I had received the green light: the plan was a go. We were to commence "Operation Safe Harvest" at 18:00 hours and carry out the mission "pie any means necessary."

By 18:07 the "Anti-Genetix" BBB cell had penetrated the tight security perimeter, and we were surrounded by dozens of the world's corporate and socio-political elite. This year's annual "State of the World Forum" enjoyed an attendance of 900 individuals from 103 nations and tribes, at a cost of a mere $5,000 per ticket. It is perhaps the classic example of liberal, consensus, win-win, Clinton-esque, spin-doctor, sell-out, cultural appropriation, commodification-of-dissent type of event in the world today.

We were indistinguishable from the other suits in the room, and we probed the reception for our target while drinking wine and chatting with heavy politicos and corporados from across the globe. As the reader can imagine, it was all quite surreal. Shapiro was nowhere in sight, so when the reception ended, we proceeded to the banquet hall for a lovely dinner. After a welcome from Mayor Willie Brown (who has turned San Francisco into a safe haven for big business and development) and remarks from the forum's moderators, Time, Inc. Chairman Emeritus Reg Brack began the keynote addresses. Brack launched into an ode on the triumph of capitalism over communism, information-age technology over real communities and the natural world, Reason over the forces of Darkness, blah blah blah. A few hisses emanated from the audience when Brack celebrated the giant retail book superstores spreading across Amerika and the online book chain www.amazon.com for selling books through cyberspace. His cold, steel-blue eyes gazed imperiously over the assemblage via two enormous video screens. The speech was met with resounding applause.

Next, the moderator introduced our man, Bob Shapiro, as a great progressive and a pleasure to have at the forum. Cautious applause mingled with murmurs of dissent, perhaps because there were people inside and outside the event distributing copies of the special "Monsanto Files" issue of *The Ecologist* magazine.

After thousands of copies of *The Ecologist* were printed, Monsanto's people got to the printshop and managed to scare them so badly that the printers shredded the entire print run rather than face the wrath of the Genetix Bad Boys. *The Ecologist* apparently managed to find a printer with a spine, and dozens of copies were express mailed to San Francisco, arriving just in time to make the event. The presence of a protest outside by concerned citizens against Monsanto was felt inside as well.

This was the moment of truth in the theater of modern pie warfare. Shapiro stepped to the stage and delivered a speech that couldn't have been crafted better by Monsanto's public relations firm Burson-Marsteller itself (the wonderful people who have repeatedly greenwashed the dirty laundry of many filthy corporations and governments). But then again, the speech most likely was written by them.

I could barely contain myself, the tension was so great. Shapiro waxed grandiloquently about Monsanto's crucial role in saving the Earth from soil erosion, pollution, overpopulation, famine, and the destructiveness of industrial society. I kid you not. He described the inherent wastefulness of cars and other industrial products, especially agricultural. His solution: more technology.

At this point, my eyes began scanning the table for any remains of the scrumptious chocolate cake we were served for dessert, and I almost leaned across the table and grabbed a slice with the intention of storming the stage right then and there perforce. Luckily, the intensive training I've undergone as a BBB field operative clicked in, and I restrained myself by sticking my hands under my buttocks and diverting my gaze away from his wild eyes, which were darting to and fro across the Big Brother screens.

Finally, he finished his speech and left the podium in a hurry. I perceived Agents Custard and Lemon Meringue approaching him directly, so I prepared for a delicious case of culinary comeuppance. As Caesar said from the banks of the wide river Rubicon, while gazing across at Rome, "The pie is cast."

A young man at a table near the stage stopped Shapiro cold in his tracks with cries of "shame, shame!" A dialogue ensued, then from Shapiro's three o'clock angle two pies originating from suited figures went airborne. The first made delightful contact with his upper left facial quadrant and left eyeglass piece, while the second sailed past harmlessly. Our victim directed some verbal unpleasantries toward the rapidly departing flan-ers, then barely stopped to wipe his glasses and face before returning to the argument, exclaiming loudly: "Roundup is perfectly safe!"

One of the moderators stepped to the microphone to introduce none other than Anita Roddick, the Body Shop global consumer conquistadora, who desperately needs some pastry treatment herself. Meanwhile, Shapiro continued to make a scene, but his handlers quickly took him by the elbow and hustled him out while wiping his head with a towel... a scene your humble correspondent will never forget, one that would cheer the hearts and souls of millions across our lonely planet. I found inside my own breast a peace which passeth all understanding.

Agents Custard and Lemon Meringue were last seen making quick strides through a side exit door, with security in hot pursuit. The rest of the BBB foot soldiers managed to escape at staggered intervals. We later found out that our comrades were detained and arrested, but even the notoriously brutal San Francisco Police Department managed to crack a laugh: "Hey, it's those pie people again!"

And so, with that I close this faithful account delivered to you after quite an eventful night, having run out of reserves of adrenaline and proper black tea.

Jim Torrey's Pastry Surprise

BY THERESA KINTZ
A.K.A. AGENT CHERRY RHUBARB TART

In December 1998, Eugene, Oregon, Mayor Jim Torrey was targeted by the Cascadia branch of the BBB. The mayor was presiding over a local public relations event on the 50th anniversary of the UN Universal Declaration of Human Rights.

Torrey had personally presided over the June 1st Tree Massacre and Pepper Spray Jamboree, where Eugene Police used massive amounts of tear gas and pepper spray on nonviolent activists during an action to protect heritage trees.

Agent Cherry Rhubarb Tart was charged with the incident, along with BBB Agent Cowpie.

In June 1999, I was arrested for perpetrating a pastry assault on Eugene's Mayor Jim Torrey. As part of my sentencing, the district attorney demanded that I sign a letter of apology their office had written for Torrey, repudiating my delicious act of criminal mischief. Instead, I've decided to submit my own.

Dear Mayor Torrey:

All I can say is I am sorry.

I'm sorry I missed when I hurled that pastry projectile, an all-American apple pie, in your direction at the ceremony where you were due to receive a decidedly undeserved human rights award. I'm sorry Bobby Lee deflected the delivery of the tasty treat I considered to be just desserts for the torture of the June 1st forest defenders by your police force. I deeply regret not practicing my pie-throwing skills more, as my defective aim prevented me from properly executing the act of culinary comeuppance that you so richly deserved.

For all of this, I most humbly and sincerely apologize. To help make amends, as an exported Eugene anarchist, I've decided to lend my support to the Eugene Anarchists for Torrey and become their representative in Wales. I wholeheartedly support their platform that every good revolution needs a Torrey.

In closing, I'd just like to say, sticks and stones may break your bones, but a pie is just flour, sugar, water, and fruit for fuck's sake.

Get over it!

Wilson "Ironbar" Tuckey
Fed a Taste of His Own

BY J.

Wilson "Ironbar" Tuckey is the epitome of a red-necked politician (his nickname is "Ironbar" on account of he once bashed some Aboriginal fellas with an iron bar in the pub he owned). A Minister for Forestry and Conservation, Tuckey had suggested that if we are to keep any old-growth forests in Australia, we would need to import giraffes because, "They are the only animals that can graze from the tree tops." In the Autumn 1999, he came to my hometown, Albury, which is a smallish regional community with about 45,000 people, to open a conference of forest fuckers from around the world.

The night before the conference, I baked a vegan custard and pear tart, with plans to slap Tuckey one if given the opportunity. My friends and I greeted the various delegates in the morning with a pretty typical "forests for life not profit" banner. There were about nine of us, and the police presence was intense. Private security firms, acting on behalf of the organizers, had briefed the local police about the prospect of attacks on the forestry equipment that was being displayed. When the police were greeted by nine locals with a banner, they sighed and let their guards down. I had by this time put my pie in a trash bin, certain that I would not be able to get within spitting distance of Tuckey. I had actually given up for the day and returned to the local environmental center, when a couple of my mates came rushing in: "He's on the lawn drinking his morning tea." I rushed out, gathered my pie, and began to move toward him.

I was intercepted by a Protective Services cop (kinda like the Secret Service), who tried to block my path to Tuckey. I kept talking shit to the cop, being a smart arse, and making him mad. My strategy worked, and I was able to get him to become so fixed on me that he didn't realize that I had backed him up almost on top of Tuckey. I started swaying from side to side as if to find a way around him. He followed. I got a rhythm happening and moved the opposite way to what our dance suggested I should do next. The cop moved where he was supposed to, leaving a nice big gap. That was when I whipped out the pie and slapped Tuckey a nice one to the side of the head.

Cops dived on me from everywhere. I was handcuffed on the ground, while Tuckey had his fists up in a boxing stance yelling at the cops: "Let him up, come on, let him up." His handlers had to physically remove him from the scene. Needless to say, I was lying on the ground laughing, handcuffed, while the world went crazy around me.

Frank Loy Gets a Pie in the Eye

On November 23, 2000, two women infiltrated the US delegation's press conference at the COP6 climate conference in The Hague, Netherlands. One was armed with a pie and the other with a mega-rant about the people struggling for climate justice globally whose voices were not being heard by conference delegates. As Frank Loy, head of the delegation, began to peddle his usual bollocks, Agent Cherry Pie scooped a rather mushy black forest gateau out of her bag, leapt forward from her front-row seat, and planted it right in his face.

Immediately, Agent Sushi jumped up onto her chair and started ranting. As Agent Sushi was carried and thrown out, ranting all the way, both agents managed to get out the door, walk past the running cops, and escape into the night.

Frank Loy, meanwhile, looked like a total mess, with pie exploded all over his face. He tried to scrape his dignity together, managed a few words, and then canceled the press conference.

Lessons to learn from this action: It is really easy! You can do it too. Just get a smart suit, a pie, think up a rant, and away you go. Keep believing you can get away with it. People are so shocked that you can use the confusion to your advantage in order to get away. Keep ranting, and they will be desperate to get you out of their precious private space, may throw you out, and then you can try and escape.

photo by David Hoffman

Clare Short and the Pie that
Fell from the Sky

Clare Short, Britain's International Development Secretary and a governor of the World Bank, was custard pied on March 5, 2001, in recognition of her disservice to the world's poor.

Just Desserts, or *Dim ond Cwstard* in Welsh, pied her when she visited Bangor in northwest Wales. She was delivering a lecture on globalization at the University of Wales, when three local patisseristas presented her with custard pies in Short-crust pastry, made with fair-trade bananas and local organic ingredients. Short is believed to be the first government minister on Earth to have received a special cabinet pudding.

Baked to a new recipe, the pies have been christened the Short-crust Bananas Turnover, to mark both the minister's political volte-face and the madness of her current globalization policies.

Short was doubtless pleased to note that after the pieing there was a marked trickle-down effect, as her clothes were enriched by the same commodities that had been imported into her face.

Short's first reaction to her pieing was to shout at the camerawoman: "Stop that woman. Don't let her get that film out." The film did get out, but Short's news managers were quickly onto editors, raising the question of "permission to film the meeting."

Bjorn Lomborg Pied for Spewing Anti-Environmental Sentiments

Danish anti-environmental author Bjorn Lomborg received his just desserts on September 5, 2001, in Oxford, England, courtesy of a fellow writer enraged at Lomborg's "dangerous and misleading" statements on crucial green issues.

Lomborg's heavily promoted book, *The Skeptical Environmentalist*, claims variously that consumer waste isn't a problem, that species loss is minimal, and that it is far too expensive to do anything about global warming.

Pie-man Mark Lynas said he was unable to ignore Lomborg's comments on climate change. "I wanted to put a Baked Alaska in his smug face," said Lynas, "in solidarity with the native Indian and Eskimo people in Alaska who are reporting rising temperatures, shrinking sea ice, and worsening effects on animal and bird life."

Many countries in the global South are also experiencing the effects of climate change. In Africa, Lake Chad is now a fraction of the size it was in the 1950s, potentially leaving millions without water. The Pacific island nation of Tuvalu is planning the evacuation of its entire population as sea levels rise.

"And yet despite all this evidence," comments Lynas, "Lomborg feeds right into the agenda of profiteering multinationals like Exxon. I don't see why the environment should suffer every time some bored, obscure academic fancies an ego trip. This book is full of dangerous nonsense."

photo courtesy Undercurrents

Pies for Bertie Ahern's Lies

BY AGENT MEDIA TART, IRISH DIVISION, BBB

"AT THIS RATE, CIVILIZATION WILL NOT END WITH A BANG, OR EVEN
A WHIMPER, BUT THE SQUISHY *SPLAT* OF A PIE."
—*IRISH EVENING HERALD*

In April 2002, I pied the *Taoiseach* (Prime Minister Bertie Ahern) in Sligo, Eire, and I still get the giggles every time I think of it. The gasp of horror from the crowd of lackeys when they saw the cream hit his gob, people ringing radio stations whinging about the lack of respect for our democratically elected leader, the big front-page splash of said leader with pie dripping down his face.

Really funny articles in the newspaper, with quotes from neighbors saying, "She seemed like such a quiet girl." I get to say completely true things live on the radio about our water table being poisoned by Coillte—the Irish Forestry Board. Coillte's monocultures are mostly in the uplands, and the toxic sprays it needs to keep its alien plantations alive seep into the waters below. There is less wildlife in Coillte's "forests" than in the town centers. As prime minister, Ahern is responsible for the actions of this semi-state company.

Blossoming all around, Spring is bursting into life. There are two yellow wagtails nesting in the bush outside the front door. Anyday now, their babies will be cracking through. A curious robin flew in yesterday for a peek at the funny nest the two-legged ones live in. A fallen tree we begged the landlord not to chop up has, to his surprise, blossomed full-leaved. Dandelions, tadpoles, red beetles... It's all exploding.

This might be the last Spring this copse sees. A road is being built through here. The compulsory purchase is done, the route marked, all the locals brainwashed into thinking it's necessary. And of course it is necessary, for them. For their civilization. For their religion: progress.

The Irish are slowly throwing off the shackles of Catholicism only to embrace an ideology equally as destructive. Old women on the bus nod, "It's great to see the country doing so well." And the young cling to their mobile phones and Nike sweatshirts. It's all wonderful, this European Union money bringing us up to date, in line with the rest of Europe. Who's laughing at us backward paddies, now that we've got cafés and cable television?

Meanwhile, for those with eyes, the misery and destruction goes on. After years of the Common Agricultural Policy, where farmers are given huge subsidies to cram loads of sheep onto every bit of land, there is nothing growing on our mountains. Here in the northwest of Ireland, the hills stand stark and bald, apart from the large swathes of sitka spruce monocultures.

Although once common land, these are now "owned" by Coillte (ironically this means "forest" in Irish). Coillte has poisoned our water table and reduced all our common land to arid, toxic tree farms.

Across the country, you see nothing but cows and sheep. Hardly any wild patches, few woodlands, ever-decreasing birds and animals. A real wet desert.

My hometown sprung up around a river, and until about 10 years ago, it was relatively unspoilt. But a big timber merchant expanded all the way down the river, ripping up hedgerows, blocking off access to the river, and erecting huge steel fences. The river died a slow, ugly death, but the townsfolk don't care since they've got river-view apartments and a health food shop now.

They've well and truly swallowed the lie of progress all right. Most of them were delighted at the pieings—politicians are easily scape-goated for all the unpleasant things the moral majority doesn't want to face up to—like garbage collection fees, incinerators, and super dumps. They want all of the baubles but none of the mess. Few of them seemed to get the real point of the pieings—that the politicians are just front men for big business and so deserve no respect.

If it even just "sows the seed in slavish men" (as an Irish activist from a century ago put it), then it was worth it.

Or as John Mitchel, a 19th century revolutionary, said, "Let the canting-fed classes rave and shriek as they will—where you see a respectable, fair-spoken lie sitting in high places, feeding itself fat on the Earth's sacrifices—down with it, strip it naked, and pitch it to the demons...
resting never 'til the huge mischief come down and the whole structure of society along with it."

Pie Any Means Necessary 58

Pie-rect Action II:
Sell-outs, Snitches, and the Like

"On les aura, nom de dieu. Que qui peut puisse!"
Loose English translation: "We'll get them, dammit.
Let those who can, do it!"
—SLOGAN OF MONTRÉAL'S *LES ENTARTISTES*

The vast majority of pastry victims have been pied for obvious reasons. Yet, pie-slingers sometimes launch attacks not just against obvious targets but against leftist authoritarians, sell-out leaders, fake environmentalists, the media, and snitches. The BBB believes that this tactic is one of many effective ways of addressing these jerks, and this section includes some good examples of how and why it is done.

The Would-Be Eco Spy

BBB operations fall into two categories. Some are meticulously rehearsed actions involving extensive reconnaissance of the battleground, comprehensive dossiers on the target, and multiple-variable combat scenarios.

Other actions are spur-of-the-moment, seat-of-the-pants affairs that only come off successfully due to good fortune and the rigorous training through which we put our field agents. "Operation Mid-Snitch," in which the BBB delivered full facial treatment in the form of three pastry projectiles to Earth First! nemesis Barry Clausen, falls into the latter category indeed.

The would-be infiltrator appeared at the site of an anti-logging action at the conclusion of the Earth First! Round River Rendezvous (RRR) in the San Juan Mountains of southern Colorado in July 1999. Shortly before they left for the RRR, agents were contacted by the General Command of the BBB, who had received a request from the BBB-Culebra (Colorado) cadre for some heavy-duty patisseristas to provide security at the event. Agents Frosty and Apple-Mulberry had just finished a training course at our Secret Ovens, Practice Range, and Headquarters deep within the Headwaters forest. They eagerly accepted the task and left immediately, armed to the teeth with the finest pies our ovens can produce.

Clausen, video camera in hand, was recognized while attempting to pry information from a young forest defender at the road blockade. Activists confronted him with ridicule, which sent him scurrying to his car and back to the town of San Luis. As our brave brigadiers followed him at a discreet distance, they concocted a creamy recipe for his just desserts. With little time for culinary perfection, and their luscious weapons left behind at basecamp (for which they were later reprimanded at a BBB post-action recap session), three pies were quickly acquired at a local shop.

As Clausen snitched away on a pay phone, the pie militants launched a delicious salvo of edible missiles: chocolate, banana-marshmallow, and lemon cream... Triple Sploosh! "Mr. Clausen, that's assault!," rang out as the spy was pied. The comment referred to a fantastic March 2, 1999 *Wall Street Journal* article ("Clausen's 'Eco-Probes' Draw Suspicion, but He Still Turns Up on TV, in Papers) that shows up Clausen for the charlatan he is and in which the joker justifies his addition of pie-throwing to a file on eco-terrorist incidents by claiming that it is an assault.

A grimacing Clausen frantically pursued the brigadiers to no avail, as they left him a mess and made a clean getaway. He finally appealed to the local police station, ranting and raving that "Earth First! got me! They hit me upside the head with a rock and broke my sunglasses!" However, the sight of cream dripping from all sides and his cheesy, "I'm undercover, don't fuck with me" shades intact didn't lend credibility to Clausen's case in the eyes of the sheriffs— who were plum tuckered-out after dealing with the biggest mass-trespass they had ever seen during the EF! action. A group of EF!ers recognized Clausen from their jail cell and proceeded to heckle and cajole the pie-laden private dick until he was forced into a humiliating retreat back to the pay phone. Clausen was overhead saying, "The Earth First! bitches got me!," which of course fueled the raucous laughter already bubbling out of the assembled crowd. Our Man Barry hung up the phone, toweled off, and drove off into the sunset to his "North American Research" office in California.

Agent Frosty issued a crisp warning to any agents of repression in our midst: "As long as spies lie, the pies will fly!"

For more information on Clausen's nefarious career of misinformation, contact the *Earth First! Journal* at www.earthfirstjournal.org.

An excellent analysis of the "Wise Use" anti-environmental movement can be found on the Clearinghouse on Environmental Advocacy and Research website at www.ewg.org/pub/home/clear/clear.html. For more information on Barry Clausen, run a search on the website for "Clausen."

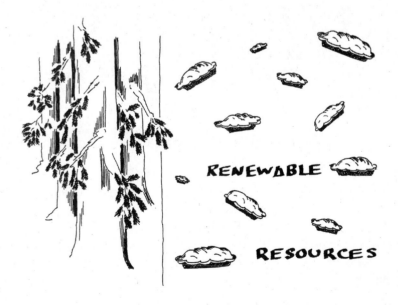

RENEWABLE

RESOURCES

Greenwashing Guerrillas Pay a Visit to Mark Moody Stuart

On October 9, 2002, Sir Mark Moody Stuart, leader of Business Action for Sustainable Development (BASD) and former chairman of Shell, was both pied and "greenwashed" by the Greenwash Guerrillas in a spectacular double whammy.

Moody Stuart was arriving for a panel discussion at St. James Church in Piccadilly, when two protesters accosted him, one wielding a cream pie and the other a tub of "greenwash." The protesters hastily dispatched their loads before running off into the night, chuckling heartily.

photo by Adrian Arbib

The protesters, calling themselves the Greenwash Guerrillas, accused Moody Stuart of "greenwashing" big business. Greenwash is when corporations use misleading information to makes themselves appear to be more socially and environmentally responsible in the face of alarming evidence to the contrary.

Despite promoting himself as Mr. Corporate Social Responsibility, Moody Stuart heads BASD—the lobby group largely responsible for wrecking the Johannesburg Earth Summit.

A Genoíno Tortada
(The Great Tortada)

What follows is an English translation of the manifesto from the Confectioners Without Borders action at a Workers Party (PT) press conference in Porto Alegre, Brazil, in January 2003, as well as background to the incident. The action: a pie in the face of Jose Genoíno, the president of the PT. The name Genoíno is close to the Portuguese word for "great," *genuína*, hence the play on words and an explanation for how the action came to be called the Great Tortada.

~~~~~~~~~~~~~~~~~~~~~~~

To compliment the actions taken this afternoon, the International Association of Confectioners Without Borders addresses the public to say that we repudiate the confusion promoted by the PT that wishes to make us believe that our movement, or the movement of movements, can be represented or incarnated in some type of government. We address the public to say that the wave that carries the PT to electoral success is not, in any form, the same wave that lifts the movement against capitalist globalization. Our movement is without leaders or representatives. No one can speak in our name. If someone in Davos represents™ the movement, it is ourselves, the thousands that occupy the roads of Geneva in protest against the reunion of bankers, businessman, and governments that the PT legitimates.

The hope for change that we carry cannot one more time be co-opted and frustrated by politicians and political parties that wish to promote themselves at our expense. This time we are going to do things differently.

In the spirit of Larry, Curly, and Moe, we greet the politician Jose Genoíno.

That all politicians leave!

A world without leaders is possible.

~~~~~~~~~~~~~~~~~~~~~~~

Before talking about throwing a pie at the president of the PT at the World Social Forum (WSF), we'll have to give some background about the situation here in Brazil and also about the WSF.

Since the presidential election in 2002, the PT has revealed its true central-right position, as opposed to the leftist position it campaigned with. After the elections, the party simply continued with the same policies and politics of the previous government of neoliberal Fernando Henrique Cardoso's party—increasing taxes, making deals with the International Monetary Fund, encouraging other South American countries to sign the Free Trade Area of the Americas (FTAA), electing the ex-president of Bank Boston as the president of the Central Bank, and as if that weren't enough, talking about giving the Central Bank unprecedented autonomy to do whatever it wants. All of this pisses lots of people off—not only anarchists but also the more radical parts of the party itself.

Back to the WSF: The forum was created in 2000, with a proposal to create a counter-forum to the World Economic Forum held annually in Davos, Switzerland. The idea was to get together all of the various movements, groups, individuals, and non-governmental organizations to discuss the creation of another world (thus the slogan: "Another world is possible"). The forum took place in Porto Alegre in southern Brazil—a city long governed by the PT and well-known for that. Unfortunately, the PT's influence in local government gave the party huge influence as to how the forum would be organized. It used the forum to promote itself in any way possible, ignoring one of the principles of the forum—that no politician would attend and participate as a politician. Politicians would only be able to participate as political individuals.

In early 2003, the WSF ignored its own principle, and invited the newly elected president, Luís Inácio Lula da Silva, to speak, as the president of Brazil, at the forum. The speech was to take place hours before he got on a plane to Davos. The true purpose of Lula's trip, as our respectable president from the PT revealed at the press conference just before receiving the pie in his face, was to make deals with the G8, talk about the FTAA, and ask for a partnership with the U$A.

Of course, Lula would never come before thousands of people and say that. It's much easier for him to say that he's going to Davos to represent the social movements and to tell all of the bad people how bad they are. We don't need to tell you that this is enough of a reason to throw a pie on someone's face, but why Genoíno? Why not Lula himself? Easy. We'd be killed by the thousands of "PTistas" who love their president no matter what stupid thing he's doing.

To finish our story, we'll tell you that we, the "Bakers Without Borders," got together for a whole night and baked our best pie with cream and strawberries. Then we went to the hotel where Genoíno was giving his press conference about Lula's business in Davos. Courage, and the heat of the ovens, filled our hearts! We threw our pie on his face and told him: "Lula doesn't represent us in Davos! The people in the streets represent us!"

A Jolly Good Show

This time around, the pie-throwing flan-archists of the BBB targeted a corporate media reporter responsible for spewing misinformation about massive anti-war protests in San Francisco.

Phase I of the BBB's "Operation Shock & Awe" began at 7:00 p.m. on March 20, 2003. In the middle of a blockaded Market Street in downtown San Francisco, outraged individuals surrounded KTVU Channel 2 reporter Jennifer Jolly (seriously, that's really her name), a typically blonde-haired, fancy-dressed TV "news" personality, and confronted her regarding her lies and blatant propaganda in support of the war in Iraq. Earlier in the day, these individuals had watched Jolly report that demonstrators were violent, disrespectful, and lawless, that parents should not bring their children to anti-war demonstrations, that she had not witnessed any incidents of police brutality, and other such garbage.

photos courtesy SF Indymedia

BBB Agent Tarte Classique, who was carrying around cans of whipped cream and paper plates, worked through the throng, announced "Pies for your lies!," and deposited a large plate of cream straight onto Jolly's talking head.

Of course, Jolly is just a cog in the corporate media machine. This phase of the BBB's "Operation Shock & Awe" was meant to address not an individual telling lies but rather an entire corporate-industrial complex. Those governing the media conglomerates also sit on the board of directors for the military weapons manufacturers and all of the other industries in an interlocking directorate of power. So, it is not really accurate or enough to just say, "The corporate media is biased." In point of fact, the corporate media *is* the war, is the military, is the destruction of the environment, is the gentrification of our cities, is the criminalization of the poor and non-aryan and foreign-born. It is everything that we loath about this society.

The BBB doesn't expect pies to stop the military. But we will use them to subvert the dominant paradigm as an auxiliary activity to the more pressing ones, such as militant demonstrations, blockades, and occupations.

We Can Be Disobedient...

Volunteers from the BBB landed a multi-layered cream and strawberry pie in the face of Luca Casarini just before he was to speak at the feminist bookstore, Bluestockings, in New York City's Lower East Side on May 4, 2003.

Casarini is the self-described "leader" of the *Disobbiedienti* (a current of the Italian anti-capitalist and anti-war movement that was once popular but is now not so sweet due to half-baked behavior on the part of its leader).

The doughy Pie-zano was frosted successfully on his way into the bookstore where a crowd had gathered to hear a presentation on anti-authoritarianism and academia. Casarini made one good point in a talk the previous night— the movement is now as globalized as capital. One consequence of this is that self-styled "leaders" will be held accountable for their actions and cannot escape by touring new territories and "re-branding" themselves. This action was a gentle reminder that those who speak like anti-authoritarians but behave like vanguardists will receive their just desserts. No flake out!

~~~BBB ACTION FLYER~~~

Why Pie Casarini?

To hear Luca Casarini speak, you would think that he represents a radical, democratic, and egalitarian part of the Italian movement. But by his actions, Casarini contradicts these ideas and his practices have alienated a large part of the Italian movement, including many previously close to *Tute Bianche*. Fortunately, much of the Italian multitude is politically sophisticated enough to refuse Casarini's will to power.

So, why pie Casarini? Unlike Subcommandante Marcos, Casarini is not an intellectual or an anti-authoritarian (contrary to the title of this event).

Former self-defined "leader" of Italian Northeastern squats.

Former self-defined "leader" of *Tute Bianche*.

Still "leader" of *Disobbiedienti*.

We believe we can be disobedient without leaders!

Stop trying to dominate globally...

• By taking over other groups' actions (especially anarchists in Torino and the rest of Italy).

• By disrupting the Bologna Social Forum and by trying to lead workers in Tuscany—and ending up being chased off by them!

• And here at Bluestockings, a feminist bookstore—not a place for macho leaders!

The Fisher King Remains at Large

For a host of reasons, the BBB rarely publicizes the incidents where we promised pie in the sky and couldn't deliver. But for the purposes of this practical BBB cookbook, we are obliged to disclose to the reader that patience is often an important ingredient in the GPU. For instance, we originally planned on pieing San Francisco Mayor Willie Brown on election night in 1998, but after hours of unsuccessfully chasing him around town, we chose instead to flan our backup target, Supervisor Gavin Newsom.

We've tried to pie a certain billionaire *four times*, and each time we have failed. Three of those times, he didn't show up at events where he was expected, and the fourth time we staked out his mansion at 7:00 a.m., only to be chased away by security guards.

So, here's the communiqué we wrote ahead of time in anticipation of pieing the man known as "the Fisher King." Your day will come, Don!

For Immediate Release

In yet another effort to stem the tide of corporate crime flooding the globe, the BBB delivered a message to the white-collar corporate crook Donald Fisher.

According to the *San Francisco Bay Guardian*, "the Fisher King" is "the most influential power broker in town." Scion of a family worth eight billion dollars, Fisher has done as much to promote privatization, downsizing, deregulation, corporate tax breaks, "free trade," and globalization as any other American businessman.

Fisher founded "The Gap," the multinational monoculture clothes chain, in 1969 and capitalized on "the generation gap" by commodifying counterculture into a profitable enterprise. Since then, he has become northern California's developer extraordinaire, and he has profited off the "income gap" even more than the generation gap. Through his enormous political influence, Fisher has received lucrative sweetheart development deals from city, county, and state officials, including his close crony Governor Pete Wilson.

As a member of the US Trade Representative's Advisory Council for Trade Negotiations, he helped to promote and develop the North American Free Trade Agreement and the General Agreement on Tariffs and Trade.

Fisher has complained that Big Business pays too much tax to support such superfluous things as schools and social programs. "I think it's time that the mayor and the board of supervisors should give something back to the business community," he said. This struck a chord with us, and since our influence with the mayor and the supervisors seems to have waned as of late, we decided to give something back to the business community ourselves. One of our pies read on the tin: "Don, you wanted the whole pie for yourself—here ya go!"

Pied Beauty

Glory be to God for splattered things—
For pies of couple-color in a banker's face;
For pecans all in stipple on a shaven cheek;
The tart which glides to haughty frown on wings;
Schemes plotted and performed, pies baked and placed;
And all who throw them, blessed are the meek.

All things counter, original, spare, strange;
Whatever is smeared or scattered (who knows how?)
Pies swift, slow, sweet, sour, cruelty free;
Thrust forward whose trajectory's past change:
Praise BBB.

—GEORGE MONBIOT
WITH APOLOGIES TO GERARD MANLEY HOPKINS

The Tale of Willie Brown
and the Cherry Pie 3

"We are free from today... Paralyze the country, you are your own leaders. Do or Pie."

—M.K. GANDHI

"Operation Free Willie"

The BBB successfully delivered a "three strikes and you're out" message to San Francisco Mayor Willie Brown in the form of three pies flopped directly in his face on November 7, 1998. Brown had just begun to deliver the opening speech at the "Great Sweep III" event, proclaiming that "this morning we have something even more dramatic to talk about," when three BBB agents tossed tofu cream, mixed berry, and pumpkin pies, all of which scored a direct hit.

"The BBB pied Mayor Willie Brown in order to expose this event for what it is: the start of the 'Great Homeless Sweep.' The mayor's 'San Francisco Cares' program is designed to drive homeless people out of key tourist and commercial districts, and last night the homeless sweeps began. Former Mayor Frank Jordan's 'Matrix' program lives on, only now with a spin-doctored smiley face. It breaks my heart to see San Francisco suffer the ravages of economic cleansing. The people have tried everything they could think of to stop the city's cruelty toward the dispossessed, but the BBB believes that if at first you don't succeed, pie pie again," said Agent Tarte.

The three pie-slingers were immediately tackled by security and police, injuring one BBB operative in the process. She was hospitalized and suffered from a broken clavicle. The BBB would later press assault charges against the person responsible. All three operatives were led away by the police.

"With the election of Democrat Gray Davis as governor, the *San Francisco Bay Guardian* stated that Brown may now be the most powerful politician in the state. The BBB conducted 'Operation Free Willie' because we believe that somewhere in the depths of Willie's soul burns the flame of compassion and justice, and we wanted to free him from the iron grip that corporate criminals, landlords, and developers have on him. If we fail in this task, then Slick Willie Brown will be remembered in the same vein as Slick Willie Clinton: a shuckster for big business and white collar crime who pretends to believe in democratic values," Agent Tarte further commented.

"Operation Free Willie" marked the conclusion of the 21st anniversary of International Pie Week. This incident marked the fifth successful pie mission of the month for the BBB.

Homelessness in San Francisco is in a crisis state. According to the National Coalition for the Homeless, there are more than seven homeless persons for every available shelter bed. Approximately 1,150 people are turned away from the largest shelters each month. The three largest shelters run nightly lotteries for beds.

Under the mayor's new "San Francisco Cares" program, the police would offer shelter to homeless people. If a person "refused" the generous help of the San Francisco Police Department, they would be ticketed for "Quality of Life" infractions!

An escalating homeless and housing crisis left a record 157 homeless people dead on the streets of San Francisco last year. The *San Francisco Examiner* quoted Brown as saying, "I'm almost to the point where I think people should be swept off the streets."

The Cherry Pie 3 Trial Begins

January 11, 1999: At 9:00 a.m., the "Cherry Pie 3" will begin their trial for the pieing of Willie Brown. Outside the courthouse at 11:00 a.m., the BBB will hold a press conference and support rally, and they will serve pie and coffee to homeless San Franciscans. "Let pie and justice be served," announced Agent Cobbler of the BBB.

The defendants—Rahula Janowski, Justin Gross, and Gerard Livernois— each face one year in jail if convicted.

"The aggressive way that District Attorney Terence Hallinan is prosecuting this case is unprecedented and clearly politically motivated," said defense attorney Katya Komisaruk. "The district attorney's normal response to protesters is to require them to do community service in exchange for dropping the charges, but in this case, Hallinan is seeking serious convictions and jail time."

Defense attorneys filed a motion to disqualify Hallinan and his office from prosecuting this case. "Hallinan's close involvement with Brown makes it impossible for him to be impartial," said defense attorney Kim Malcheski. Hallinan's involvement with Brown began 35 years ago when Hallinan spent two years as the volunteer coordinator of Youth for Brown, campaigning for

Brown's first bid for the California State Assembly. The pie-throwers' motion to recuse Hallinan was denied.

Pie Trial Defense Can't Send in the Clown

January 15, 1999, from the *San Francisco Chronicle*: Three defendants on trial for a pie attack on San Francisco Mayor Willie Brown said yesterday that they were sorry he got hurt in the incident but not that he got creamed.

The three said that hitting the mayor in the face with a pie was a legitimate, nonviolent political prank designed to ridicule Brown's policies on the homeless.

Defense attorneys had been counting on bringing in a professional clown to testify about the obscure history of political pie pranks in Europe and the US during the 1960s. But Superior Court Judge Ernest Goldsmith barred that testimony, along with that of an advocate for the homeless, after the prosecution objected.

The rulings subdued what had been a circus-like atmosphere at the trial, which is expected to end today. Through it all, the defendants did their best to portray what happened as a joke that got a little out of hand.

"It's comedy, you know. Its intent was to be humorous," Justin Gross testified of the attack, which resulted in a melee that left Brown with a sprained ankle and a bump on his knee.

"I'm very sorry for the injuries that happened in the excitement after we pied the mayor," said Gross, who, along with Gerard Livernois and Rahula Janowski, faces charges of misdemeanor battery and assault on a public official.

All three testified about their concerns regarding animals, the homeless, and other causes. A parade of character witnesses attested to their honesty and nonviolent approaches to social justice issues.

Gross said that he had picked the Civic Center event, a trash pickup day known as "Great Sweep III," to commit the pie assault because it symbolized the "great homeless sweep" Brown was planning.

Janowski told jurors that she works with Food Not Bombs to feed the homeless. "I feel kind of a moral obligation to do things I can to make the world better," she said.

"I wanted to place a pie in Willie Brown's face to cause some humor and to cause some reconsideration of his projected homeless policies."

She said she feared that the mayor was working to "criminalize" homelessness by cracking down on habitual drunks. In fact, the mayor and police did enact such a plan.

"I think it's a terrible policy," she said.

Prosecutor Maria Bee zeroed in on whether the pie assailants should have known that the attack would have caused a commotion that could lead to injuries.

Janowski said it "never crossed my mind" that "either the pie recipient or the pie-er would be injured." Janowski suffered a broken clavicle when she was tackled by a friend of the mayor.

Livernois' testimony delved more into the mayor's policies on other issues, including a proposed Mission Bay academic project that Livernois believes will be used for animal research projects that he opposes.

Livernois has previously said that the mayor was pompous and "out of touch," statements highlighted by the prosecutor. "In fact, you wanted to bring the mayor down a notch?," Bee insisted.

Livernois maintained that he wanted to "open dialogue" on the issue of homelessness in the city.

Livernois also explained the significance of Hamlet the pig in the scheme of things. A defense attorney had shown witnesses a picture of the animal Wednesday, without going into the pig's role.

Livernois testified that he had seen the pig at the Great Sweep III, where Hamlet was serving as a mascot, and he was worried about it. He told a police captain that it was roaming free.

"I wanted to make sure it was attended to," he said, adding that he had seen the animal featured Monday on a television program honoring "America's Greatest Pets."

The Pie is Cast

When Brown testified against the three homelessness activists who had thrown pies at him, he repeatedly urged the court to make an example of the defendants. The trial ended in a split verdict. The jurors deliberated for more than nine hours,

finally acquitting the defendants of the heavier charge of assaulting a public official, while convicting them of simple battery. On February 24, 1999, Judge Goldsmith complied with the mayor's demand, sentencing all three pie-throwers to the maximum penalty of six months in the county jail.

Spectators who managed to get a seat in the crowded courtroom voiced their disapproval as the draconian sentences were pronounced. Even Janowski was sentenced to six months, despite the testimony of the mayor's friend Garland Rosario that he tackled her in the wake of the pie-ing, snapped her collar-bone, and created a permanent disability. Janowski's attorney, Katya Komisaruk, told the judge that this sentence was a *shanda fur die goyim*, an embarrassment for the community.

All three defendants and their attorneys made statements in court before Goldsmith issued the sentences. Gross said simply, "Poverty is violence." Livernois focused on the continuing disastrous impacts of the mayor's policies toward the homeless community. And Janowski pointed to the similarity between the rhetoric of some of San Francisco's civic leaders and that of Nazi Germany's Ministry of Propaganda. After Goldsmith issued the first six-month sentence, the packed courtroom went silent, and Livernois replied: "You're insane, your honor."

The BBB remains undeterred by the case's outcome and issued the following communiqué in response to the harsh sentences: "The pie is cast. We shall not rest until justice, as well as dessert, is served."

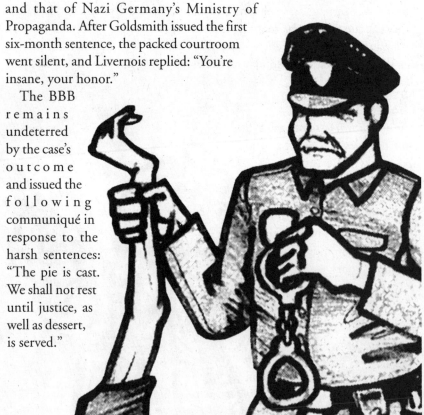

The Cherry Pie 3
Sentenced to Six Months in Jail

Sentencing Statement Read by Rahula Janowski

February 25, 1999: Today in San Francisco, a large number of people are participating in a 21-day fast as a part of the "Save the Dream Campaign" organized by Religious Witness. The dream referred to is the dream of Presidio housing for homeless people, as recommended by the voters of San Francisco when Proposition L passed in 1998.

photos courtesy Whispered Media

While Willie Brown doesn't have ultimate authority over the use of the Presidio, he does, as one of California's most powerful politicians, have influence that he could use to try to make that dream come true. So far, he hasn't, and hundreds of people will be fasting to show their commitment to humane and respectful treatment of homeless people.

In all honesty, I doubt that Brown will be swayed to advocate for homeless people in any way. I plan to participate in this fast because we must have hope, and we must engage in a variety of activities to secure justice for the poor and homeless among us.

In the years I have lived in San Francisco, I have watched the number of homeless people increase at a heart-sickening rate. I've seen vacancy rates plummet as rents rise drastically and affordable housing goes the way of the dinosaurs. Hand in hand with this housing crisis, I have seen many of our public officials respond in a cruel way by criminalizing homeless people. The repressive program known as the Matrix did not end when Brown was elected, it simply became a nameless policy of harassment. Where is the compassion, the humanity, in our collective response to this situation?

Brown began his political career as a tireless campaigner for civil rights. When activists staged sit-ins in the '60s to fight racial discrimination, Brown was there, lining up legal support for the hundreds of arrested activists, among them our current district attorney, Terence Hallinan. Throughout his political career, Brown has maintained his commitment to civil rights for African American people, which has won him support and a loyal constituency. This makes it all the harder to bear when we see him ignoring and denying the civil rights of homeless people.

There is a famous quotation from Holocaust survivor Pastor Niemoeller. I'm sure you're familiar with it. It begins, "First they came for the Jews, and I did not speak out because I was not a Jew." It concludes, "Then they came for me, and there was nobody left to speak out for me." What this famous and moving quotation does not mention is that before they came for the Jews, they came for the homeless, the mentally disabled, the unemployed, and all those categorized as "asocial."

The rationale behind the purge of poor and "asocial" people in Germany was as follows: "The psychological importance of a planned campaign against the nuisance of begging should not be underestimated. Beggars often force their poverty upon people in the most repulsive way for their own selfish purposes. If this sight disappears from view, the result will be a definite feeling of relief and liberation. People will feel that things are becoming more stable again and that the economy is improving once more." The similarities between this rhetoric from Nazi Germany's Ministry of Propaganda and our own local

officials in their fight to rid San Francisco of visible homelessness is obvious. Let me be clear—I am not accusing Brown or anyone else of being a Nazi. I am simply pointing out that by forgetting or ignoring that aspect of the Nazi Holocaust, we are in grave danger. As they say, those who ignore history are condemned to repeat it.

The few people protesting the scapegoating of our homeless community are ignored. In one of his first acts as mayor, Brown canceled a much needed summit on homelessness, claiming it was a problem that couldn't be solved. Homelessness can be solved, but it will take honesty, integrity, bravery, and a commitment to putting human needs ahead of economic profiteering. When our elected officials are so firmly in the pocket of wealthy interests, it is hard to be optimistic about change.

Throwing a pie at Brown was a political act, an act of political theater intended to hold him accountable for the harm he does as mayor to homeless people and to draw attention to the plight faced by poor and homeless people in San Francisco. The aggressive prosecution of this case by Brown's longtime friend and political ally, District Attorney Terence Hallinan, has been politically motivated. As stated by Brown here in this courtroom, we were to be made examples of.

And examples we are.

We are examples of how the justice system can be discretionary and discriminatory—how politics and power brokering affect an individual's opportunity for fair treatment under the law.

Our case is also an illuminating example of the lack of perspective and proportion in our society today. To treat pie-throwing as a violent act and to prosecute it so aggressively is ridiculous beyond all measure.

It is apparent to me that the real crime we are to be sentenced for is the crime of rocking the boat, challenging the status quo, and irritating one of the state's most powerful and influential politicians. The crimes committed against homeless people on a daily basis in this city consistently go

 unpunished. Homeless people are regularly assaulted, their belongings are stolen, and their civil liberties are consistently violated.

I can only hope that a day will come when crimes against the dispossessed and the powerless are prosecuted as thoroughly as crimes against the ruling class. For that day to come, the values held by our society must be dramatically altered. The most basic of human needs must become more important than greed.

I know that the act of throwing a pie alone will not bring about this change. However, it is my hope that as the people of San Francisco look at our action and its aftermath, they will become more aware of the disparities of our governmental, criminal, and judicial institutions. And it is my hope that, as they become aware, they will be moved to act. That they will say, "No More!" and work to dismantle this unjust, compassionless, and humorless system.

Judge Goldsmith Says a Few Words

The sentencing of a convicted defendant seeks to accomplish three things. First, to punish the defendant. Second, to dissuade or deter the defendant from engaging in similar criminal behavior in the future. Third, to dissuade or deter others from engaging in the illegal behavior. Ms. Janowski, Mr. Gross, and Mr. Livernois, it is the court's responsibility to deter you and others from committing similar illegal acts, and the imposition of punishment is the only means at the court's disposal to accomplish this. In all of your communications and statements, you have voiced sentiments suggesting that you will continue this behavior. The only thing the court can do is to make the punishment such that you and others will be deterred. Consider that there are some 500,000 elected officials in the US. They are senators, councilpersons, mayors, a president, school board members, and so on. Disagreement with public policy, no matter how heartfelt, sincere, and perhaps even correct, does not give license to commit battery or any other crime upon a person or such officials.

There is a mortar that holds this democracy together and that is our system of elections. Americans need not take to the streets, grab weapons, or hit someone if they disagree with policy or their side loses an election. Americans know that there will be another round at the ballot box in a year, or two, or four. Your side has a chance of winning next time. The result is stability almost unknown elsewhere in the world, and most of us would like to keep it that way.

Political, social, and economic issues coalesce within the electoral system within this country. As citizens you can walk precincts, call voters, and work to elect those with whom you agree. Indeed, you can aspire to run for office yourselves and have the forum to try to effect political change. Arching over all of this are our rights of expression and free speech.

You have alluded to these rights in connection with your actions, which you should learn from the jury verdict, do not include battery. You do, however, have the right to assemble, to peacefully seek media coverage, to demonstrate publicly with certain bounds, to form and speak before citizen's groups in order to develop and articulate your views, to support or deny support to elected officials, and to disseminate information to convince others. You could have exercised those rights on November 7, 1998.

In order to exercise your rights of protected speech and assembly, to enjoy the freedom of expression supported by the constitution, you must do so without violence. You are free to attack an elected official's policies; you are not free to attack his or her person.

The defendants in this case rejected probation. Probation which means a promise not to commit crimes. Punishment by sentences to county jail are the only means available to the courts to impress upon the defendants and others that the acts for which the defendants were convicted are not sanctioned but are against the law and will not be tolerated.

At this point the judge asks if arraignment for sentencing is waived and sentences each defendant to the maximum six months in jail.

Would You Do It Again?

BY RAHULA JANOWSKI

I always thought if I went to jail it would be for something really serious, like blowing up the Pentagon or an extreme act of sabotage. And yet I found myself in jail, having sabotaged nothing more than a little man's big ego. At times, I have been overwhelmed by the sheer silliness of it all, and I have laughed right along with other inmates when they found out why I was in the San Francisco County Jail.

But there were other times—hard, depressing times. I missed my friends, my community, my home, my life, and I was bitter about what seemed to be an exorbitant price to pay for having put a pie in Willie Brown's face. I kept several mental talismans on hand for those times.

I would think about Mumia Abu-Jamal, who has been in jail for more than 15 years now and looking death in the face each day. I would think of the MOVE prisoners, who are doing time because a cop was killed by "friendly fire" and whose sister, Merle, died in jail. I thought of the Chinese dissident who is spending the rest of his life in jail for having thrown paint on a poster of Mao during the Tiennamen uprising in 1989. I also thought about my bunkie, Marlo (name changed of course), in jail for some drug thing with her kids in foster care. Nobody ever came to visit her, nobody put money on her books, there was no one to accept her collect calls. And her situation was far from unusual.

Being in jail sucked, but I had it good. Every form of support I could hope for was available to me, and I knew my community was waiting to welcome me with open arms. I was constantly reminded that my community supported and cared for me. In addition to letters and books, there were donations so that I could use the phone and buy vegan treats from the commissary. I had visits every weekend. I was still able to have political dialogues, keep track of all the gossip, and maintain my relationships.

I don't, however, believe that my situation was all right simply because other people have it worse. It's perfectly clear that my co-defendants and I went to jail not for what we did but for who we did it to. The injustice of that is not so much that we went to jail but that this one man has rights and protections that so exceed those of regular people, including the rights of retaliation.

With few exceptions, the response of other inmates when they found out why I was there was positive. I got a lot of laughter and high fives, and a few people said I "shoulda used a brick." For the most part, what impressed people was not the politics. It was that I'd had the audacity to "attack" someone famous.

I would have much rather discussed any of the political issues that led to me being in jail, but despite what I may have thought previously, talking politics in jail isn't all that easy. Practically everyone in jail knows the system is fucked, the government and the police are corrupt, and that the deck is stacked against poor people and people of color.

Like many of my comrades, I had romanticized imprisonment, thinking that doing time would make me a better person in the process and I'd radicalize all or many of my fellow inmates. The truth was, however, that I had far more to learn than to teach. I have some clear ideas about the evils of the systems we live under, and some thoughts on what to do about it, but the realities of what the system does to those on the bottom is a bit mysterious.

I found that a major difference between activists and other folks isn't our understanding of how the world is fucked up. It's a matter of hope. On the occasions that I was able to have political conversations in jail, I found that many people saw no point in agitating for change. When I think about the view of history gained in public schools, I can understand why resistance seems futile. In my years of schooling, I never heard anything about social justice movements. If people knew that struggles have succeeded in the past, they would be far more inclined to think there's a point to struggling now.

Spending time in jail, it becomes easier to understand why many people (people who've done time) obey authority figures. There are many opportunities to defy authority in jail, particularly in a program such as the one I was in where inmates are never out of the sight of at least one deputy. The rules are petty and much of the discipline reduces inmates to the role of a child. In disputes between inmates and deputies, the senior deputies always took the side of the deputy (hardly surprising), so it was clear that any act of defiance simply led to harsher punishment for the inmate.

At least 75 percent of the people I met in jail were there on probation violations. On its face, probation generally seems like a better choice, allowing people to continue with their lives rather than going to jail. But probation is a trap that many people are caught up in and is used by the criminal justice system to keep people under control. I met many people who, by violating their probation numerous times, had spent more time in jail than they would have spent if they'd just taken a jail sentence from the start.

Having already done the deed, gone through trial, and been convicted of battery, my comrades and I faced the choice of three years of probation (along with fines and community service) or a maximum six-month jail term. We refused probation, and I am firmly convinced that was the best choice we could have made. Had we accepted probation, for three years we would have been unable to participate in any activities that could have resulted in arrest.

This would have effectively prevented us from participating in protests and direct actions, in addition to a total loss of civil liberties—being subject to search at any time, which would have included our homes and any home or vehicle we were in. Any contact with a police officer could have meant a probation violation. By refusing probation, I ended up having a very intense and illuminating four months, at the end of which I was (am) free to do what I choose, as much as anyone is. Based on my experience, I would say that there are times when it is definitely better to do the time and be done with it than to be under far more stringent state control for a much longer time.

I do have two regrets. One of them is that I got brutalized and my collarbone was broken. The other is that I didn't use a cream pie. In retrospect, I would say that a cream pie should always be a pie-throwers choice because of the thorough facial coverage and the immediate comprehension of bystanders. While this may sound flip, it is honest. Through the whole court process, I learned. Through the time I spent in jail, I learned. I learned through experience what I had known on an intellectual level: that the courts are corrupt and the systems of power are completely intertwined.

I learned that, although I have been economically poor all of my life, I am privileged and not only on the basis of my skin color. I am privileged because I was somehow raised to trust myself and to expect to be treated with respect. If every person expected and demanded to be treated with compassion and respect, no one would stand for this shit called capitalism.

In addition to all of the things I learned in jail, being totally removed for four months forced me to re-examine my life, my goals, and my beliefs. Ever since I became politicized I have been running from one project to the next, giving my all, trying my hardest to learn on the run, and to be as effective as possible. In jail, I found myself questioning: Have I been effective? Is my community effective? Can I keep this up without going crazy or burning out? What exactly do I want to accomplish and am I going about it the right way? I didn't answer all of these questions. Having asked them, though, I find that I keep asking them, keep reflecting on them, and will continue to do so. The fact that it took me a month to learn to communicate with fellow inmates made me realize in a very concrete sense how isolated the radical social justice community can become, and I'm convinced that to be effective, isolation needs to be overcome.

"Would you do it again?" *No! Hell no!* Once was enough! But I don't regret it, and I wouldn't take it back. Although many aspects of the entire experience—from the actual pieing to court process and the jail time—were pretty darn unpleasant, at every step I learned. I learned as much and grew as much in four months in jail as I had in the proceeding two years of constant struggle and organizing, and  now that it's over I can say unreservedly that it was totally worth it.

While I wouldn't choose to replicate this experience, I don't mean that I would refrain from taking actions that would potentially lead to jail time. In general, activists tend to avoid taking large risks, which imposes restrictions on our effectiveness. It has been said (by people with limited imagination) that pieing is a violent act. Yes, throwing a pie certainly crosses the lines of traditional nonviolent civil disobedience, but in light of the lack of numbers that social and environmental activists face today, perhaps that line needs to be crossed more often. One of the best results from the media exposure that pieing has received is not just that more people will pie corporate and political criminals but that people will realize there are more options available to activists than the "tried and true" tactics of yesterday. I hope people will be inspired to become more creative, to be original, and to not be bound by the tactics of our predecessors.

My advice to potential pie-throwers is this:
•Use a cream-based pie,
•If at all possible, don't get caught,
•If faced with the choice of a relatively short jail sentence (under a year) or probation, go to jail, and
•Remember: Jail sucks. But inaction sucks more. If you take no risks, you gain nothing.

Pie-Hurler's Diet Leads to New Vegan Era at Jail

SAN FRANCISCO—For many Americans, a meal without meat or dairy products would be considered cruel and unusual punishment.

But a handful of lentil-loving inmates at the San Francisco Jail are thrilled about Sheriff Michael Hennessey's decision to be the first in the state to put vegan food on a jail menu.

The change in policy comes after much letter-writing on behalf of Gerard Livernois, who was jailed in February for lofting a pie in Mayor Willie Brown's face.

Hennessey initially denied Livernois' request for vegan food, but he came around last month after hundreds of pro-vegan e-mail messages and letters fell on his desk.

"I've got to admit to my own ignorance about vegetarianism and the depth of commitment that people have to this," Hennessey said. "From what I've since learned, I'm convinced that their beliefs are sincere and they're not trying to manipulate the system."

Livernois' attorneys say San Francisco is the first county in California to serve vegan food to its inmates and one of the first in the nation.

"People running most jails think they only have to provide religious diets, and that's not true," said Livernois' attorney Derek St. Pierre, explaining that vegans had equally strong "ethical beliefs."

Starting as early as December, according to Sheriff's Department officials, the jail's food supplier will offer a steady vegan option.

Hennessey said he had come around after receiving letters and phone calls from vegans, with e-mail coming from as far away as Switzerland and Italy. Hennessey also heard testimony from his own staff. One of his social workers is a vegan, and an assistant sheriff is a vegetarian.

Not that the sheriff is ready to change his own ethical beliefs.

"I just had a Polish sausage for lunch," he said. "I'm from Iowa. I have a long history of being carnivorous."

—*SAN FRANCISCO EXAMINER*, JULY 3, 1999

Gay Nuns "Cream" Homophobic Preacher
Solidarity Action with the Cherry Pie 3

An offshoot of ACT UP San Francisco, a controversial direct action organization, pied supporters of Reverend Fred Phelps on March 26, 1999. Dessert was served by a duo known as the Pieing Nuns as Phelps and his clan held a rally, complete with signs such as "AIDS Kills Fags," to protest Mayor Willie Brown's officiating at a mass domestic partners ceremony at City Hall.

In defiance of the six-month jail sentences for the BBB agents who pied Brown, two activists dressed in nun's habits and tossed four vegan and organic banana tofu pies into the hate-twisted faces of Phelps' entourage as part of "Operation Second Phelping." Citing the heinous attacks on queers nationwide and the repression of political pie protest in San Francisco, Sister Agents Thelma and Louise demanded that community members respond with anger and power to this very real and immediate threat.

"Queers have been tossing pies since Anita Bryant's homophobic attacks on gays and lesbians in the late 1970s. The venom spewed forth by Phelps and his ilk is no different," stated Sister Thelma. "From the vicious stabbing of Robert Hillsborough in the Mission District 20 years ago to the slaying of Henry Northington, whose decapitated head was found impaled on a Virginia bridge, the hatred remains. We must confront these religious hypocrites and let them know that we will no longer be their victims. It is imperative that the gay community unite to protect our safety and well being."

The dynamic duo stated that they pied Phelps in solidarity with two groups—first, the "Cherry Pie 3" pie-litical prisoners. Secondly, this operation went out to BBB Agent Creamy Genes, who gave geneticist Neil First a delicious gift of a cream pie in the kisser.

The Pieing Nuns are also critical of the gay mainstream's fight for gays in the military and domestic partners legislation, as well as the refusal to aggressively challenge the climate of gay violence heating up around the country. Furthermore, these smokescreen solutions do nothing to address critical issues facing rural gay communities, such as legislation that ensures fair housing, equal employment, and adequate health care.

Denouncing "gay marriage" as a sell-out agenda by straight society to conform queers to a heterosexual norm, Sisters Thelma and Louise call such platitudes ineffectual, creating the illusion of progression while the validation of hate-motivated attacks against gays and lesbians increases.

It's Not Just Pies, Anymore

"O, pardon me, thou bleeding piece of earth,
That I am meek and gentle with these butchers…
Cry 'Havoc,' and let slip the pies of war."
—WILLIAM SHAKESPEARE

It's Not Just Pies, Anymore
FOOD THROWING

Pies are just one item that political pranksters use to throw, push, or dump onto the personage or property of a scoundrel. Roman historians recorded disgruntled citizens pelting Emperor Nero with onions in the Coliseum shortly after the Common Era began. In Greece, an ancient custom still exists whereby a citizen may legally pour yogurt on a politician, as long as the citizen does not resort to employing foul language in the course of the act! Noël Godin began a long and illustrious anarchist career by dumping a bucket of glue on a Portuguese politician in protest of the country's military dictatorship and brutal repression of dissidents. Rotten eggs, tomatoes, cow dung, and even cat litter have been employed to great effect in many lands. A few of the finer incidents from recent times are listed below, in the words of the participants. Don't get any ideas, mind you!

Late 1980s

Amsterdam, Netherlands—A big anti-racist rally was organized to take place on Dam Square. The reason for the manifestation was the mounting anti-immigration sentiments in the Dutch society and government, fomented by an evermore racist Fortress Europe/European Union. So it was quite a surreal experience for the thousands of participants at the manifestation to see Prime Minister Wim Kok step onto the stage to start a speech. Before long, some unknown objects started heading toward him, but the public clearly had not prepared itself for this situation. Luckily, around the corner was situated the famous (now defunct) anarchist eco-grocery "De Spruitjes" in the former squat-building NRC-gebouw.

People started to run there to collect some objects such as eggs and tomatoes. This must have inspired others because within a few moments— and with the glad collaboration of the Spruitjes people—there was a whole delivery-chain between the shop and the square and more and more food items filled the sky. Fruits and vegetables were now being brought in by the crate, and the stage and speaker were being severely covered. At the end, almost the whole organic content of the shop had been transferred toward the stage. The conclusion was that it is not always most efficient to throw pies to politicians—sometimes the single ingredients serve the purpose better.

AS A POLITICAL ACT

July 1996 and October 1996

Vancouver, Canada—At the 11th International AIDS Conference, ACT UP coordinated the "Vancouver Bloodbath," a controversial action that garnered international recognition. During the demonstration, angry activists stormed a keynote pharmaceutical address on anti-viral therapies. They doused drug company-funded researchers Margaret Fischl, Paul Volberding, and others with fake blood. ACT UP criticized the conflict of interest that impedes progress to determine a cure for AIDS and demanded that AIDS research focus on strengthening the human immune system rather than killing a virus.

San Francisco, California—ACT UP again gained international attention by staging an action against a multi-million dollar corporate giant, the San Francisco AIDS Foundation, for its acceptance of drug company money to promote harmful, experimental pharmaceutical products. Screaming activists dumped 25 pounds of used kitty litter on Executive Director Pat Christen, whom the community referred to as "Fat Cat Pat" due to her inflated salary.

Ronnie Burk, pictured in the photo above, became an active member of ACT UP after hearing about the Vancouver Bloodbath. A passionate activist and wicked fellow, Ronnie passed away just before this book went to print. His spirit and work continues on with ACT UP San Francisco.

February 10, 1998

London, England—At the British Music Awards, Danbert and Alice of Chumbawamba "decide to have a quiet word with British Deputy Prime Minister John Prescott," intent on steering the conversation around to New Labor's despicable treatment of the 500 sacked Liverpool dockworkers. Only a few days earlier, the dockworkers had been forced to end their picket and accept a derisory pay-off.

The bucket of ice water that had been left at Prescott's feet was too tempting.

Danbert carefully aimed the whole thing at our Great Leader's Understudy, and with the words, "This is for the Liverpool dockers," poured the whole lot on his New Labor suit. "His tie was ugly, anyway," Danbert said later.

March 6, 2000

Prague, Czechoslovakia—Anarchists egg US Secretary of State Madeleine Albright for her war crimes.

May 2000

There's something about Dan Glickman. In late 1996, Secretary of Agriculture Dan Glickman was in Rome, Italy, for a conference on food when naked protesters threw non-genetically modified soybeans at him.

A few months later, he was at a public meeting with a group of politicians in Montana when a woman—protesting the killing of bison that stray from national parks—threw a bucket of rotten buffalo guts at the speakers. This included Glickman, two US senators, and the governor of Montana.

Pie Any Means Necessary 94

In May 2000, during a hearing at the House of Representatives, a man upset about shipments of contaminated soda to Eastern Europe threatened to kill himself and smashed two bottles, showering the room with glass and carbonated soda as Glickman and two stunned officials sat a few feet away.

Shortly thereafter, a member of People for the Ethical Treatment of Animals ran onto the stage at a government nutrition meeting in Washington, DC, and threw a tofu cream pie at Glickman's face, yelling: "Shame on you, Dan Glickman, for pushing meat and promoting animal cruelty."

But why is it that people want to throw stuff at Glickman? "People take my love of food too seriously," he said. That must be it!

June 2000

Pamplona, Basque Country, Spain—Michel Camdessus, former International Monetary Fund general director, was received in Pamplona with an egg full of red paint that colored his face and clothes (as well as those of his wife and the university rector).

Camdessus came to Pamplona after being invited by the private and famous Opus Dei University to a seminary called "External Debt, Problems, and Solutions." The action was taken by the group "Painters Without Borders."

October 6, 2000

Kitchener, Canada—A protester threw chocolate milk at Stockwell Day, the leader of the Canadian Alliance, just as he was outlining his party's platform for the next election. Day left the stage for a few minutes, returning with a new shirt, tie, and a few wisecracks.

"Boy, if there's any time I needed a wet suit," he said, referring to a recent interview he did that critics later complained was more about image than substance. After having won a recent election, Day roared up to a news conference in a watercraft and skin-tight outfit.

January 9, 2001

London, England—Prime Minister Tony Blair faced a barrage of rotten fruit and took a direct hit from a tomato thrown by demonstrators protesting Britain's policy toward Iraq.

The tomato smashed into his back as Blair entered the City of Bristol College to open a new campus. Blair's assistant wiped the mess from his jacket, but the tomato attack left a large, red stain on his right shoulder.

The protesters lobbed more tomatoes and other fruit, including small, rotten oranges, but the projectiles missed the prime minister. Police held back two dozen demonstrators as they surged toward Blair.

The demonstrators didn't limit their protests to the Iraqi situation. Also on hand was a group from Farmers for Action, who led the fuel tax protests that nearly brought Britain to a standstill in September 2000. The farmers brought along a dozen tractors and trucks, but police stopped them short of the city council offices where Blair was to give a speech.

May 9, 2001

Seoul, South Korea—Protesters threw raw eggs at US Deputy Secretary of State Richard Armitage as he was driving to a round of meetings with South Korean cabinet ministers.

At least six activists were arrested after pelting Armitage's car with eggs as he was driving out of the Grand Hyatt Hotel, witnesses said.

The Reverend Mun Jeong-Hyun, a leader of a group that objects to US plans for a global missile defense system, said, "We're not happy with this coming to Korea." According to Mun, "Armitage is trying to force Korea to accept the US missile defense program."

March 14, 2001

Lublin, Poland—Two anarchists bombarded European Union (EU) President Romano Prodi's limousine with eggs and shouted slogans against the EU.

May 16, 2001

Rhyl, Wales—British Deputy Prime Minister John Prescott was attacked and wrestled to the ground after punching an egg-throwing demonstrator. Prescott, the British political equivalent of a US vice president, lashed out in response to being hit in the face by the egg, which had been thrown at close range from a crowd of angry protesters. The ugly fracas capped a day where the launch of a Labor Party manifesto was overshadowed by senior politicians facing public abuse and hostility.

A man hurled the egg at Prescott on his way to the Rhyl theater. Television footage showed Prescott turn and jab the egg-thrower.

The man lunged at Prescott across a crowd-control barrier, and the pair became locked in a struggle that resulted in Prescott being pinned to the ground. Prescott was held there for several seconds before four police officers and two Labor officials could separate the two.

The local Conservative candidate promptly called for Prescott to resign. Brendan Murphy, standing in the Vale of Clwyd, said: "What sort of role model is Prescott for young people? Throwing eggs is almost a time-honored tradition in this country. It might hurt and sting your face a bit, but it doesn't harm you. If politicians can't put up with things like that, they shouldn't be in the job."

The man who threw the egg was later identified as Craig Evans, a "countryside contractor," who was described by his girlfriend as "a placid lad who had never been in trouble."

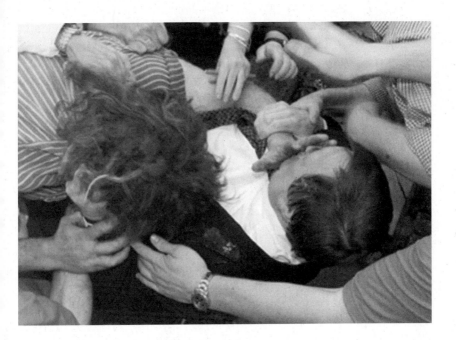

The raw egg is a common form of political protest in Britain. "There is a long and honorable tradition of throwing eggs at politicians," said Malcolm Rifkind, the leader of Scotland's Conservative Party.

May 17, 2001

Warsaw, Poland—Former US President Bill Clinton was jeered by anti-globalization protesters and attacked by an egg-throwing anarchist while he was visiting Poland's capital as part of a European speaking tour.

According to reports, the president laughed at the matter, saying, "It's good for young people to be angry about something nowadays."

May 26, 2001

Bristol, England—A top man from the Socialist Worker Party (SWP), Alex Callinicos, got a politician's welcome in Bristol at the Resistance Conference. He must have thought that the SWP was getting in with the anti-capitalists and everything was going to plan.

Inspired by the egging of Prescott, the opportunity was too good to miss—and neither did the eggs! The obvious first question from the floor was: "Are we gonna let the SWP parasites dominate the anti-capitalist movement?!"

July 24, 2001

Vancouver, Canada—At 5:00 a.m., Translink Chair George Puil received a delivery of one ton of fresh manure. The load was placed outside of his home in Kitsilano with a sign that read, "Hey George, the Bus Strike Stinks—Day 145."

"This transit strike really stinks," said Agent Cowpie of the Biotic Bullshit Brigade. "We're laying the bullshit right where it ought to be, on the steps of the man responsible for it: George Puil."

"The smelly excuses of Vancouver politicians are no longer good enough," said Agent Crappy. "We will continue to take action until they start acting like adults rather than the bickering, privatizing, excuse-making weasels that they are!"

September 5, 2001

Nottingham, England—The revolting British Shadow Home Secretary Ann Widdecombe (pied earlier in the year at an anti-racist protest) had to dodge more missiles. She had come to Nottingham to talk about homelessness. As she entered a building, a passing cyclist narrowly missed her ear with an egg. Once inside, a woman—incensed at the Tory swine who had said that the "fairest way to deal with refugees was to put them all into reception centers"—stood up, ranting: "You mean prisons don't you, Ann, you racist scum? Have you ever been to prison? Do you have any idea how people suffer?" She flung two eggs, one hitting the rostrum and splattering all over Ann's suit. The woman was nicked by the Special Branch to prevent a breach of the peace, but she was released a couple of hours later after Widdecombe left.

photo courtesy EBS

September 6, 2001

Edmonton, Canada—Three members of the Edmonton Edible Ballot Society (EBS) were charged with eating their ballots in the last federal election. The charges followed a year-long investigation by Elections Canada into the group's activities.

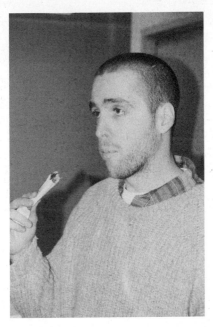

photos courtesy EBS

Marika Schwandt was alleged to have liquefied her ballot with soy milk and fruit before drinking it, and Mike Hudema reportedly sauteed his ballot in a tangy stir fry. Witnesses claimed that Chad Blackburn ate his ballot raw (clearly Chad is a masochist with an iron stomach).

Approximately 100 members of the Edible Ballot Society ate their ballots at polling stations across Canada during the last election.

The trio ate their ballots because they refused to participate in a system where casting a vote for some lying tool once every four years passes for democracy. The EBS wanted to draw attention to the shallow nature of the procedural electoral process and to spark dialogue on participatory alternatives.

November 7, 2001

London, England—It was a cold evening at the packed Hackney Community College canteen, where people gathered for a discussion on "How Clapton Can Benefit from Regeneration." In reality, this meeting was nothing more than a public relations exercise by Hackney Council.

The head of the Regeneration Committee is Guy Nichollson—and guess who was on the panel trying to feed a sugar-coated regeneration pill to the packed room! At least two women from the community had heard enough and decided to tell him just what they thought regeneration had accomplished. They walked to the front of the room, and while one told the audience that they were about to make a special presentation to Nichollson, the other searched the buffet for cream cakes or pies... but they had all been scoffed!

Realizing a vegetable samosa wouldn't have the desired effect, she grabbed an enormous handful of mayonnaise, walked over to the target and aimed. Bullseye! Nichollson sat there looking bewildered with egg mayonnaise dripping down his face and onto his pullover.

August 7, 2002

Szczecin, Poland—Several thousand shipyard workers stormed the Odra clothes factory where workers had not received pay for several months. The factory workers had been on partial strike and had stopped working for six hours a day.

The director of the enterprise was dragged out and had eggs thrown all over him. The shipyard workers performed the ritual of driving the boss out the factory on a wheelbarrow (an age-old custom in Poland when firing your boss). The police didn't intervene out of "fear to enrage the demonstrators."

March 18, 2003

Copenhagen, Denmark—An anti-war protester hurled red paint at Denmark's prime minister shortly before a press a conference where he was set to back US military action against Iraq.

Anders Fogh Rasmussen was unhurt, but he postponed the press briefing in Copenhagen. Foreign Minister Per Stig Moeller was also hit by splashes of paint in the incident inside the parliament building.

The protester—overpowered by parliament security—shouted, "You've got blood on your hands," as he was taken away.

BY DAN FORTSON

Key of Am. Am G Em
In the Heart of the redwood forest
where the ragin' rivers flow
a reckless band of outlaws
is counting up its dough.

They make delicious mischief
to heal the world of hurt
to the land of power lunches
they bring their just dessert.

Chorus
Inya face! Charlie Hurwitz
Inya face! Milton Friedman
There's poetic justice dripping from your chin.
Inya face! Bob Shapiro
Inya face! They're the people's heroes
And you're just a notch upon their rolling pin.

This band of Biotic Bakers
is out to cause a fuss.
You know their aim is deadly
and they speak for all of us.

They stand for peace and justice
cut those bigshots down to size
with a tasty lemon custard
right between the eyes.

Chorus

So all you corporados
you better watch your step
these custard packin' mamas
are gonna get you yet.

In the heart of the redwood forest
their ovens are aflame
there's an apple pie a' sizzlin,
and it just might bare your name.

Chorus

Renato Ruggiero, director general, World Trade Organization
London, England, October 1998

My, How the Times Have Changed

"Six Who Helped Shape New Corporate Landscape Find Faults"

BY ROBERT D. HERSHEY, JR.
FROM THE *NEW YORK TIMES*

The world of business has changed remarkably in the past quarter century... but amid the progress, what has been lost that was worthwhile? We asked several people who used to be at the heights of different aspects of business to assess what they regretted most about the changes that have occurred. They singled out situations ranging from the new "villainy" of globalization to the lack of real thoughtfulness now given to investments.

Following is one response:
RICHARD J. MAHONEY, former CEO of the Monsanto Company; currently Distinguished Executive in Residence at the Weidenbaum Center on the Economy, Government, and Public Policy.

Peter Allgeier, co-president, Free Trade Area of the Americas
Rio de Janeiro, Brazil, August 2003

"Americans doing business in developing countries in the 1970s, 1980s, and even into the early 1990s were generally welcome partners. We brought the desired technology, market access, management skills, and money for investment. I recall being the subject of local newspaper photo-ops to celebrate the opening of a new facility or the establishment of a technology collaboration with a local partner.

"As the 1990s progressed, however, the headlines changed from collaboration to exploitation with the appearance of a villain called globalization. To be sure, the business parties and government officials still found the agreements attractive, but opposition emerged, particularly in the 'have' countries among groups protesting the exploitation of the 'have nots.'

"Facts were not necessarily important; appearance was—the appearance of exploitation, whether in local wages paid, farm-cropping practices exported, Western culture 'imposed,' or a host of other issues that were embodied at the wild gathering of international trade protesters during the World Trade Organization meeting in Seattle in November 1999.

In the early 1990s, I received an award and an ovation following a speech I made describing the promise of agricultural biotechnology to feed the world. My successor as CEO in the late 1990s received a pie in the face from a protester at a similar forum. What a difference those few years have made."

AFTER-WORDS

AFTER

"Violence is as American as apple pie."
—Eldridge Cleaver

As this book winds its way through the editorial process, our glorious Commander-in-Thief George "the only dope worth smoking" W. Bush is about to open the gates of hell in the Middle East. The media pumps out images of powerful, violent men in suits and uniforms who are making threats and promising destruction if they don't get their way.

There has been a very clear shift in society since September 11, 2001, as if the very ground moved under our feet, and we haven't yet caught our balance. Our collective imbalance is understandable, given the stream of horrors committed globally. The USA PATRIOT Act and other state efforts to scare the shit out of people have been largely successful. Secretary of Defense Donald Rumsfeld said it all: "The American way of life is not negotiable."

So, all things considered, what now is the role of dissent? The answer is clear: Active resistance is more important than ever, and more dangerous. What forms our resistance should take are less clear.

One aspect of the BBB's campaign that distinguishes us from other freedom fighters is that our weapons of choice hurt nothing more than the image and ego of our targets. Although we don't claim to be "nonviolent" in the pro-active Gandhian sense, we do claim to be "not violent." The principle is simple: If the people pie, the leaders will swallow.

Federal, provincial, state, and local officials have all been creamed, with one California county supervisor calling it an organized "attack on government." We couldn't have said it better ourselves! How can one honestly claim that an attack on government is not entirely justified?

In a statement that clearly validates our position, Dr. Martin Luther King, Jr. once proclaimed, "If a man [sic] hasn't found something he will pie for, he isn't fit to live."

Let They Who Are Without Sin Cast the First Scone

Some historical regimes have been easier to shame into change than others. For instance, the British Empire, ruthless though it was, held public pretenses of justice and progress that liberation groups in its colonies were able to

WORDS

expose as false and thus exploit. Nazi Germany, on the other hand, held no such pretenses and could not be shamed into doing anything. It's often easier to parody a hypocritical liberal than a fascist.

Likewise, the Clinton era, ruthless though it was, could be attacked through satire in order to expose its hypocrisy. Unfortunately, there is not much that's funny about the Bush gang; they are obviously a bunch of evil oil thugs and military spooks who make few pretensions otherwise. Would it be a good idea nowadays, for instance, to pie Bush? I'd love to see it, but it wouldn't have nearly the impact that pieing Clinton would have had when he was in office. Times have changed, and now there would be a massive propaganda campaign to turn the pie into a deadly terrorist weapon and the pie-slinger into an enemy combatant who was trained at secret al-Pieda camps somewhere in Afghanistan.

Effective revolutionaries such as Emma, Che, and Marcos consistently seem to have good senses of humor— perhaps it is what kept them inspired and motivated to fight during grim times. This makes sense, given that humor and tragedy are the opposite sides of the same coin. Those with a deep appreciation of one often have a concomitant relation with the other. Militancy *and* humor can help to pull us through these grim times and stay strong.

Hold the Moral Pie Ground

Attacks on government are clearly justified. However, an incident in the Netherlands gives us reason to recognize that *"l'attentat du flan,"* or "pastry assassination," is still a serious attack.

On March 14, 2002, one of the Dutch BBB cells pied a racist, right-wing politician named Pim Fortuyn. On May 6 of the same year, Fortuyn was assassinated by a lone gunman who was an environmental and animal rights activist. He explained at his trial that he feared the rise of another Hitler and acted to protect the vulnerable people in Dutch society. This action caused a surge of violence and antipathy toward radical left movements, who were blamed indirectly for Fortuyn's death.

The anarchist collective Eurodusnie, who is associated with the pie group TAART, issued a statement in response to verbal and physical attacks made on their social centers by Fortuyn supporters: "We see that the murder of Fortuyn only increased the growing right-wing sentiments. This is yet another reason why we have no sympathy whatsoever for the murder. Fortuyn is being presented by many as a political saint, which is completely unjust. His ideas about immigration, health care, social security, and the Islamic culture remain as disgusting now as before his death. Therefore, resistance against right-wing and racist ideas remains as necessary as ever."

Where does one draw the line on what is violent and what is not? Or when is violence justified? Perhaps only the Dalai Lama, so often quoted by New Agers, dogmatic pacifists, and other confused individuals, can speak to this adequately: "*Hayagriva* is the compassionate aspect of Buddhist wrath. In other words, you do not wish to cause injury, but sometimes when people refuse to become enlightened, you must frighten them into seeing the light. Intimidation without hurting. It is sometimes the only way."

Mahatma Gandhi on Violence:
"Where the choice exists between cowardice and violence, I would advise violence. I praise and extol the serene courage of dying without killing. Yet I desire that those who have not this courage should rather cultivate the art of killing and being killed, than basely to avoid the danger. This is because he who runs away commits mental violence; he has not the courage of facing death by killing. I would a thousand times prefer violence than the emasculation of a whole race. I prefer to use arms in defense of honor rather than remain the vile witness of dishonor.
—"DECLARATION ON QUESTION OF THE USE OF VIOLENCE IN DEFENSE OF RIGHTS," *THE GUARDIAN*, DECEMBER 16, 1938

Tribute to Arbel Gal

On July 4, 2001, the "Israeli Militia of the International Pie Brigades" and Indymedia activists entered the Israeli Parliament Hall and threw a pie in the face of Communication Minister Rubi Rivilin. Indymedia had recently organized a local campaign against a plan to merge several television networks into one monster corporation that also owns all of the major newspapers and magazines.

The pie-thrower, a much-loved and respected rebel named Arbel, died afterward of a rare heart disease. Her funeral was on the one-year anniversary of the pie action. The following tribute is from one of Arbel's comrades.

Arbel Gal
1982 – 2002

artwork by Latuff

Arbel was with us since the beginning of Indymedia Israel. She was 20 years old when she died. Arbel was from Kibbutz Dalia, which is northeast of Haifa.

She was very positive, charismatic, aggressive in the positive sense, always speaking her mind, fighting for her beliefs, but she would also listen to other opinions in meetings and give people the benefit of the doubt too.

Arbel was present at almost every anti-occupation demonstration that took place, pushing the limits of the dialogue. For instance, she would sing pro-conscientious objector chants and get groups of people to join in, even though the Peace Now coordinators didn't want to speak openly about the issue.

She also did political theater. Arbel was working with a group of "actors" to do a street theater performance about Agenda 21 (which was the agenda being pushed for the Johannesburg Earth Summit), however, she died before she could perform it.

The Pies

Recipes from the BBB

BY AGENT LEMON MERINGUE

Tofu Cream Pie

Speaking from experience (three missions accomplished), I think using some variation of a cream pie is your best bet. Leaving the pie-ee with a face full of light-colored goop not only accomplishes your goal more effectively, it also communicates what's going on better. This can also help avoid situations where you get your ass kicked. Here are some excellent recipes that I still make... to eat!

Crust:
2 cups graham cracker crumbs
1/4 cup pure maple syrup
1/4 teaspoon almond extract

Preheat oven to 350. Mix all ingredients until moistened, then press into an oiled 9-inch pie dish and bake for 5 minutes.

Filling:
1 pound silken tofu
1/3 cup sucanat
1 tablespoon tahini or almond butter
1/2 teaspoon salt
2 tablespoons lemon juice
1/2 teaspoon lemon zest (grated lemon rind)
1/2 teaspoon almond extract

Blend it all up in a blender or food processor, put it in the pie shell, and let sit for an hour or two. It's super yummy and gets the job done! If you wanna make a cheesecake, just add 2 tablespoons of cornstarch dissolved in 2 tablespoons of soymilk. Bake at 350 for 30 minutes.

~~~~~~~~~~~~~~~~~~~~~~~~~~~~

Whipped Tofu Topping

1 pound fresh firm tofu
1/4 cup maple syrup
1 tablespoon vanilla extract
2 tablespoons water for blending

Blend all, refrigerate, and apply to the top of your pie with spatula or through a pastry bag.

~~~~~~~~~~~~~~~~~~~~~~~~~~~~

Egg-Free Lemon (or Lime) Pie Filling

This pie will often gel up more than you intend, which means it bounces off and doesn't achieve the optimal facial coverage. (I'm speaking from experience here. It sucks to pie and leave no trace on the person's face!) A suggestion would be to mess around with the recipe, using less of the egg replacer, or more liquid, so that it stays gooier.

1/4 cup egg replacer
1 cup sugar
1/4 teaspoon salt (optional)
1 1/2 cups hot water

1/3 cup lemon juice
2 tablespoons lemon (or lime) rind
1 baked 9-inch pie crust

In a double boiler, combine egg replacer, sugar, and salt. Stir with rubber spatula until thoroughly blended. Add water, lemon juice, and lemon rind. Continue stirring until smooth and thick. When dropped from a spatula, the pie filling should mound. Remove from heat. Stir for 5 minutes to cool. Pour into pie crust. Let cool thoroughly. Refrigerate at least 2 hours before serving.

~~~~~~~~~~~~~~~~~~~~~~~~

Pumpkin Pie

We don't particularly recommend this recipe unless you are going throw it around Thanksgiving Day in the US, because then it will fit into the holiday pumpkin pie spirit. Or, if you think there is a good chance that you will be unsuccessful in getting near your target, then if you don't throw the pie, you and your mates can go home and eat it! But again, a light-colored cream pie is really the best pie to employ in your arsenal.

1 1/2 cups cooked, mashed pumpkin
1 1/2 cups (12 oz.) tofu
1/2 cup pure maple syrup
1 teaspoon cinnamon
1/4 teaspoon nutmeg
1/4 teaspoon dry ginger
1/8 teaspoon allspice
1/8 teaspoon cloves
1/2 teaspoon sea salt
2 tablespoons water (as needed)

Preheat oven to 400. Blend all ingredients until creamy and smooth, adding the water last if it is needed. Pour filling into pre-made crust. Bake for 20 minutes.

Glaze for crust:
1 tablespoon brown rice syrup
2 teaspoons apple juice

Brush on crust, then bake 10 minutes longer.

~~~~~~~~~~~~~~~~~~~~~~~~~~~~~~~

Apple Pie

A good pie to eat. Will help keep BBB agents fueled and ready for action.

Crust:
Put 2 cups flour in a bowl. Add 2/3 cup plus a fat tablespoon extra of shortening and a 1/2 teaspoon of salt. Put that in the freezer to chill.

When it is good 'n' cold, pull it out of the freezer and use two table knives to cut the shortening into the flour.

Add approximately 1/3 cup of water (a sprinkle at a time) to the flour, stirring with a rubber spatula. Add just enough water to barely hold the flour together. Knead briefly, then cut in half and roll it out.

If you are not ready to roll out and use the crust immediately, put it back in the freezer until you are ready so that it stays chilled.

This will make enough for a top and bottom crust. Most pies will bake fine for 10 minutes at 425, then 25-35 minutes at 375.

Filling:
6 cups tart apples, peeled and thinly sliced
1/3 cup sugar
1/2 teaspoon cinnamon
1/2 teaspoon nutmeg
3 tablespoons flour
2 teaspoons lemon juice
1/2 cup brown sugar
3 tablespoons margarine, softened

Preheat the oven to 425. Roll out the pie crust and arrange in pie plate. Put the sliced apples into a large bowl.

Mix the sugar, cinnamon, nutmeg, and 1 tablespoon of flour in another bowl, then sprinkle over the apples. Toss until the slices are coated, sprinkle with lemon juice, and toss again. Pour into the pie crust.

Blend the brown sugar, margarine, and the other 2 tablespoons of flour with a fork. Sprinkle over the apples.

Add top crust, either by rolling it out and cutting air vents, cutting strips and braiding it into a lattice, or some other fancy pattern.

Bake for 10 minutes, then lower heat to 350 and bake for another 45 minutes, until the crust is golden brown.

Links & Resources

Pie-throwing Groups

Biotic Baking Brigade
www.bioticbakingbrigade.org

Pie-throwing Anarchist Noël Godin
www.mindspring.com/~jaybab/noel.html

The Great American Pieman, Aron Kay
www.pieman.org

Mad Anarchist Bakers' League
www.madanarchistbakersleague.com

Les Entartistes
www.entartistes.ca

Operation Dessert Storm
www.antimedia.net/dessertstorm

TAART
www.members.tripod.com/taart

Like-minded Groups and Interesting Links

Whispered Media (culture jammers and guerrilla media warriors from the beginning of the pie wars. Have produced a number of films, including *The Pie's the Limit*)
wm@videoactivism.org
www.whisperedmedia.org; www.videoactivism.org

Earth First! Journal
POB 3023, Tucson, AZ, 85702-3023
collective@earthfirstjournal.org
www.earthfirstjournal.org

Eco-Action (great online eco-anarchist resource, includes articles from the fine *Do Or Die* publication)
doordtp@yahoo.co.uk
www.eco-action.org

CrimeThinc
www.crimethinc.com

A-Infos News Service
www.ainfos.ca

Resist!
www.resist.ca

Indymedia and San Francisco Bay Area Indymedia
www.indymedia.org; www.indybay.org

Security.tao.ca and Security-news email list <security-news@resist.ca> (excellent resources
on all aspects of computer security and encryption "for autonomous resistance movements")

Hootenanny (lyrics, chords, and recorded radical campfire and folk songs)
www.rebelfolk.org

Undercurrents
www.undercurrents.org

Adbusters
www.adbusters.org

ACT UP San Francisco
www.actupsf.com

Free Software Foundation
www.gnu.org

Warrior Poets Society (Dennis Fritzinger's poetry brigade)
POB 14501, Berkeley, CA 94712-5501

Green and Black Network
www.blackandgreen.org

Earth Liberation Front
www.earthliberationfront.com

Animal Liberation Front
www.animalliberation.net

The Deconstructionist Institute for Surreal Topology (includes groups such as the
Edible Ballot Society and Bad Press, plus cool agit-prop and posters)
www.tao.ca/~wrench/dist

Situationist International websites
www.nothingness.org/SI; www.notbored.org/SI.html; members.optusnet.com.au/~rkeehan

Peoples' Global Action
www.agp.org

The Ecologist
www.ecologist.org

Other Titles from AK Press

Books

MARTHA **ACKELSBERG**—*Free Women of Spain*

KATHY **ACKER**—*Pussycat Fever*

MICHAEL **ALBERT**—*Moving Forward: Program for a Participatory Economy*

JOEL **ANDREAS**—*Addicted to War: Why the U.S. Can't Kick Militarism*

ALEXANDER **BERKMAN**—*What is Anarchism?*

HAKIM **BEY**—*Immediatism*

JANET **BIEHL** & PETER **STAUDENMAIER**— *Ecofascism: Lessons From The German Experience*

JACK **BLACK**—*You Can't Win*

MURRAY **BOOKCHIN**—*Anarchism, Marxism, and the Future of the Left*

MURRAY **BOOKCHIN**—*Social Anarchism or Lifestyle Anarchism: An Unbridgeable Chasm*

MURRAY **BOOKCHIN**—*Spanish Anarchists: The Heroic Years 1868-1936, The*

MURRAY **BOOKCHIN**—*To Remember Spain: The Anarchist and Syndicalist Revolution of 1936*

MURRAY **BOOKCHIN**—*Which Way for the Ecology Movement?*

DANNY **BURNS**—*Poll Tax Rebellion*

CHRIS **CARLSSON**—*Critical Mass: Bicycling's Defiant Celebration*

JAMES **CARR**–*Bad*

NOAM **CHOMSKY**—*At War With Asia*

NOAM **CHOMSKY**—*Language and Politics*

NOAM **CHOMSKY**—*Radical Priorities*

WARD **CHURCHILL**—*On the Justice of Roosting Chickens: Reflections on the Consequences of U.S. Imperial Arrogance and Criminality*

HARRY **CLEAVER**—*Reading Capital Politically*

ALEXANDER **COCKBURN** & JEFFREY **ST. CLAIR** (ed.)—*Politics of Anti-Semitism, The*

ALEXANDER **COCKBURN** & JEFFREY **ST. CLAIR** (ed.)—*Serpents in the Garden*

DANIEL & GABRIEL **COHN-BENDIT**—*Obsolete Communism: The Left-Wing Alternative*

EG SMITH COLLECTIVE—*Animal Ingredients A–Z (3rd edition)*

VOLTAIRINE de **CLEYRE**—*Voltairine de Cleyre Reader*

HOWARD **EHRLICH**—*Reinventing Anarchy, Again*

SIMON **FORD**—*Realization and Suppression of the Situationist International: An Annotated Bibliography 1972–1992, The*

YVES **FREMION** & **VOLNY**—*Orgasms of History: 3000 Years of Spontaneous Revolt*

DANIEL **GUERIN**—*No Gods No Masters*

AGUSTIN **GUILLAMON**—*Friends Of Durruti Group, 1937–1939, The*

ANN **HANSEN**—*Direct Action: Memoirs Of An Urban Guerilla*

WILLIAM **HERRICK**—*Jumping the Line: The Adventures and Misadventures of an American Radical*

FRED **HO**—*Legacy to Liberation: Politics & Culture of Revolutionary Asian/Pacific America*

STEWART **HOME**—*Assault on Culture*

STEWART **HOME**—*Neoism, Plagiarism & Praxis*

STEWART **HOME**—*Neoist Manifestos / The Art Strike Papers*

STEWART **HOME**—*No Pity*

STEWART **HOME**—*Red London*

STEWART **HOME**—*What Is Situationism? A Reader*

JAMES **KELMAN**—*Some Recent Attacks: Essays Cultural And Political*

KEN **KNABB**—*Complete Cinematic Works of Guy Debord*

KATYA **KOMISARUK**—*Beat the Heat: How to Handle Encounters With Law Enforcement*

NESTOR **MAKHNO**—*Struggle Against The State & Other Essays, The*

G.A. **MATIASZ**—*End Time*

CHERIE **MATRIX**—*Tales From the Clit*

ALBERT **MELTZER**—*Anarchism: Arguments For & Against*

ALBERT **MELTZER**—*I Couldn't Paint Golden Angels*

RAY **MURPHY**—*Siege Of Gresham*

NORMAN **NAWROCKI**—*Rebel Moon*

HENRY **NORMAL**—*Map of Heaven, A*

HENRY **NORMAL**—*Dream Ticket*

HENRY **NORMAL**—*Fifteenth of February*

HENRY **NORMAL**—*Third Person*

FIONBARRA **O'DOCHARTAIGH**—*Ulster's White Negroes: From Civil Rights To Insurrection*

DAN **O'MAHONY**—*Four Letter World*

CRAIG **O'HARA**—*Philosophy Of Punk, The*

ANTON **PANNEKOEK**—*Workers' Councils*

BEN **REITMAN**—*Sister of the Road: the Autobiography of Boxcar Bertha*

PENNY **RIMBAUD**—*Diamond Signature, The*

PENNY **RIMBAUD**—*Shibboleth: My Revolting Life*

RUDOLF **ROCKER**—*Anarcho-Syndicalism*

RON **SAKOLSKY** & STEPHEN **DUNIFER**—*Seizing the Airwaves: A Free Radio Handbook*

ROY **SAN FILIPPO**—*New World In Our Hearts: 8 Years of Writings from the Love and Rage Revolutionary Anarchist Federation, A*

ALEXANDRE **SKIRDA**—*Facing the Enemy: A History Of Anarchist Organisation From Proudhon To May 1968*

ALEXANDRE **SKIRDA**—*Nestor Mahkno—Anarchy's Cossack*

VALERIE **SOLANAS**—*Scum Manifesto*

CJ **STONE**—*Housing Benefit Hill & Other Places*

ANTONIO **TELLEZ**—*Sabate: Guerilla Extraordinary*

MICHAEL **TOBIAS**—*Rage and Reason*

JIM **TULLY**—*Beggars of Life: A Hobo Autobiography*

TOM **VAGUE**—*Anarchy in the UK: The Angry Brigade*

TOM **VAGUE**—*Great British Mistake, The*

TOM **VAGUE**—*Televisionaries*

JAN **VALTIN**—*Out of the Night*

RAOUL **VANEIGEM**—*Cavalier History Of Surrealism, A*

FRANCOIS EUGENE **VIDOCQ**—*Memoirs of Vidocq: Master of Crime*

GEE **VOUCHER**—*Crass Art And Other Pre-Postmodern Monsters*

MARK J **WHITE**—*Idol Killing, An*

JOHN **YATES**—*Controlled Flight Into Terrain*

JOHN **YATES**—*September Commando*

BENJAMIN **ZEPHANIAH**—*Little Book of Vegan Poems*

BENJAMIN **ZEPHANIAH**—*School's Out*

HELLO—*2/15: The Day The World Said NO To War*

DARK STAR COLLECTIVE —*Beneath the Paving Stones: Situationists and the Beach, May 68*

DARK STAR COLLECTIVE —*Quiet Rumours: An Anarcha-Feminist Reader*

ANONYMOUS —*Test Card F*

CLASS WAR FEDERATION —*Unfinished Business: The Politics of Class War*

CDs

THE EX—*1936: The Spanish Revolution*

MUMIA **ABU JAMAL**—*175 Progress Drive*

MUMIA **ABU JAMAL**—*All Things Censored Vol.1*

MUMIA **ABU JAMAL**—*Spoken Word*

FREEDOM ARCHIVES—*Chile: Promise of Freedom*

FREEDOM ARCHIVES—*Prisons on Fire: George Jackson, Attica & Black Liberation*

JUDI **BARI**—*Who Bombed Judi Bari?*

JELLO **BIAFRA**—*Become the Media*

JELLO **BIAFRA**—*Beyond The Valley of the Gift Police*

JELLO **BIAFRA**—*High Priest of Harmful*

JELLO **BIAFRA**—*I Blow Minds For A Living*

JELLO **BIAFRA**—*If Evolution Is Outlawed*

JELLO **BIAFRA**—*Machine Gun In The Clown's Hand*

JELLO **BIAFRA**—*No More Cocoons*

NOAM **CHOMSKY**—*American Addiction, An*

NOAM **CHOMSKY**—*Case Studies in Hypocrisy*

NOAM **CHOMSKY**—*Emerging Framework of World Power*

NOAM **CHOMSKY**—*Free Market Fantasies*

NOAM **CHOMSKY**—*New War On Terrorism: Fact And Fiction*

NOAM **CHOMSKY**—*Propaganda and Control of the Public Mind*

NOAM **CHOMSKY**—*Prospects for Democracy*

NOAM **CHOMSKY/CHUMBAWAMBA**—*For A Free Humanity: For Anarchy*

WARD **CHURCHILL**—*Doing Time: The Politics of Imprisonment*

WARD **CHURCHILL**—*In A Pig's Eye: Reflections on the Police State, Repression, and Native America*

WARD **CHURCHILL**—*Life in Occupied America*

WARD **CHURCHILL**—*Pacifism and Pathology in the American Left*

ALEXANDER **COCKBURN**—*Beating the Devil: The Incendiary Rants of Alexander Cockburn*

ANGELA **DAVIS**—*Prison Industrial Complex, The*

JAMES **KELMAN**—*Seven Stories*

TOM **LEONARD**—*Nora's Place and Other Poems 1965–99*

CHRISTIAN **PARENTI**—*Taking Liberties: Policing, Prisons and Surveillance in an Age of Crisis*

UTAH **PHILLIPS**—*I've Got To know*

DAVID **ROVICS**—*Behind the Barricades: Best of David Rovics*

ARUNDHATI **ROY**—*Come September*

VARIOUS—*Better Read Than Dead*

VARIOUS—*Less Rock, More Talk*

VARIOUS—*Mob Action Against the State: Collected Speeches from the Bay Area Anarchist Bookfair*

VARIOUS—*Monkeywrenching the New World Order*

VARIOUS—*Return of the Read Menace*

HOWARD **ZINN**—*Artists In A Time of War*

HOWARD **ZINN**—*Heroes and Martyrs: Emma Goldman, Sacco & Vanzetti, and the Revolutionary Struggle*

HOWARD **ZINN**—*People's History of the United States: A Lecture at Reed College, A*

HOWARD **ZINN**—*People's History Project*

HOWARD **ZINN**–*Stories Hollywood Never Tells*

DVDs

NOAM **CHOMSKY**—*Distorted Morality*

ARUNDHATI **ROY**—*Instant Mix Imperial Democracy*

continued from page i

Richard Wilson# (director, California Department of Forestry) in Fort Bragg, California, USA by BBB • Hedwige Nuyens (Belgian minister of labor) in Bruxelles by Collectif Autonome de Chomeurs • Carles Campuzano (Spanish congressman) in Catalonia, Spain • Ujjal Dosanjh (attorney general, British Columbia) in Vancouver, Canada • Hoops Harrison (national director, Canadian Alliance of Student Associations) in Manitoba, Canada by Balaklava Bakers • Lord David Sainsbury* (British minister of science & corporate executive) in Swansea, UK by Welsh Action Against Genetics • Pierre Pettigrew (human resources minister) in Montréal, Canada by LE • Arielle Dombasle (French actress) by IAP • Reverend Fred Phelps (homophobic fundamentalist Christian) pied twice, first time in San Francisco, California, USA by Pieing Nuns, then by BBB • Ronald McDonald (duh!) pied five times by PETA • Marie-France Botte (cop) in Bruxelles, Belgium • Jesse "The Body" Ventura (governor) in Minneapolis, Minnesota, USA • a Dayton, Ohio Power and Lights Company spokesman • Roy Rogers (cowboy musician) • Dr. Neal First (geneticist & animal cloner) in New Hampshire, USA by the BBB • Roger D. Landry (president, La Presse) in Montréal, Canada by LE • Dr. Jose

TRIED &

Delgado (fascist mind-control doctor from Franco's Spain) by Groucho-Marxists in Vancouver, Canada • Charlie Raines (confused environmentalist with the Sierra Club) in Eugene, Oregon, USA by Mad Anarchist Bakers' League • Daniel Toscon de Plantier (president, Cannes Film Society, France) by IAP • Frank Rizzo (police commissioner & mayor) in Philadelphia, Pennsylvania, USA • Guru Maharaj Ji in Detroit, Michigan, USA by Yippies • Gérald Lacoste (president, Montréal Stock Exchange) by LE • Dennis Avery (biotech industry PR man) in Grinnell, Iowa by BBB-Central Iowa Anarchists • John Herity (Environment Canada) in Montréal, Canada by LE • William F. Buckley (right-wing journalist) in New York, USA by Pieman • Alain Beverini (celebrity) in Bruxelles, Belgium by IAP • Nick Brown (agriculture minister) in London, UK • Abe Beame (former New York City mayor) by Pieman • 30 Indonesian business leaders accompanying President Abdurrahman Wahid in London, UK by BBB • Keith Campbell (animal cloner, "co-creator" of Dolly the Sheep) in Sussex, UK by BBB • Hilmar Kaba (head of Vienna's right-wing FPO party) in Austria • David Icke (British anti-Semitic conspiracy theorist & author) in Vancouver, Canada by Meringue Marauders • Jacques Parizeau (premier) in Québec, Canada by LE • Karl Lagerfeld (fashion designer) pied twice by PETA • Darryl Cherney (Earth First! activist & musician) pied three times by BBB & others • James Rhodes (governor) in Ohio, USA by Yippies • Steve Rubell (Studio 54 owner & disco culture promoter) in New York, USA by Pieman • Robert Shapiro (CEO, Monsanto) in San Francisco, California, USA by BBB • Allan Rock (health minister, Canada) in Montréal, Canada by LE • Jean Gol (Belgian economy minister) by IAP • Kenny Rogers (animal-abusing celebrity) pied three times by PETA • Daniel Patrick Moynihan (US ambassador to the UN) in New York, USA by Pieman • James Torrey (mayor) in Eugene, Oregon, USA by BBB-Cascadia • Phyllis Schlafly (right-wing anti-feminist) in New York, USA by Emma Goldman Brigade & Pieman • Willie Brown (mayor) in San Francisco, California, USA by BBB • Jerry Brown (governor) in California, USA by Pieman • Bosse Ringholm (finance minister) in Stockholm, Sweden by Tärtbrigade • Jan Wenner (editor & publisher, *Rolling Stone*) in Boulder, Colorado, USA by Pieman • Harold Rosen (councilman) in Miami Beach, Florida, USA by Yippies • Driek van Vught (socialist lefty wanker) in Leiden, Netherlands by Eurodusnie • Quentin Kopp (supervisor) in San Francisco, California, USA by Pieman • Filip Dewinter (right-wing Flemish leader) in Amsterdam, Netherlands • Carl Pope (president, Sierra Club) in San Francisco,